Audrey Fenner
Editor

Managing Digital Resources in Libraries

Managing Digital Resources in Libraries has been co-published simultaneously as *The Acquisitions Librarian*, Numbers 33/34 2005.

*Pre-publication REVIEWS,
COMMENTARIES,
EVALUATIONS . . .*

"**A**n interesting compilation of reflections on today's issues in managing digital resources. The contributions range from the theoretical to the more practical. Major emphasis is on the management of electronic journals, although a chapter on the use of PDA technology gives the collection a greater breadth in terms of formats addressed. This collection also has a global reach, addressing projects outside the United States. The range of solutions offered for handling digital resources, from various viewpoints, illustrates that no one method for managing digital materials is dominating the scene yet. The chapters addressing copyright issues, licensing concepts, and issues surrounding bibliographic control are particularly strong. The case studies address situations found in academic, health sciences, and public libraries."

Eleanor I. Cook, MA, MSLS
Professor and Serials Coordinator
Appalachian State University
Boone, North Carolina

The Haworth Information Press®
An Imprint of The Haworth Press, Inc.

Managing Digital Resources in Libraries

Managing Digital Resources in Libraries has been co-published simultaneously as *The Acquisitions Librarian*, Numbers 33/34 2005.

The Acquisitions Librarian Monographic "Separates"

Below is a list of "separates," which in serials librarianship means a special issue simultaneously published as a special journal issue or double-issue *and* as a "separate" hardbound monograph. (This is a format which we also call a "DocuSerial.")

"Separates" are published because specialized libraries or professionals may wish to purchase a specific thematic issue by itself in a format which can be separately cataloged and shelved, as opposed to purchasing the journal on an on-going basis. Faculty members may also more easily consider a "separate" for classroom adoption.

"Separates" are carefully classified separately with the major book jobbers so that the journal tie-in can be noted on new book order slips to avoid duplicate purchasing.

You may wish to visit Haworth's Website at . . .

http://www.HaworthPress.com

. . . to search our online catalog for complete tables of contents of these separates and related publications.

You may also call 1-800-HAWORTH (outside US/Canada: 607-722-5857), or Fax 1-800-895-0582 (outside US/Canada: 607-771-0012), or e-mail at:

docdelivery@haworthpress.com

Managing Digital Resources in Libraries, edited by Audrey Fenner (No. 33/34, 2005). *A practical guide to managing library materials in digital formats; examines innovations including the integration of PDA-accessible resources into collections and the development of all-digital libraries.*

Selecting Materials for Library Collections, edited by Audrey Fenner (No. 31/32, 2004). *A comprehensive overview of building, maintaining, and updating any library collection.*

Collection Development Policies: New Directions for Changing Collections, edited by Daniel C. Mack (No. 30, 2003). *An in-depth guide to building and maintaining effective policy statements.*

Acquisitions in Different and Special Subject Areas, edited by Abulfazal M. Fazle Kabir (No. 29, 2003). *Presents profiles, methods, and processes for acquisitions in specialized subject areas, including local and regional poetry, oceanography, educational information in electronic formats, popular fiction collections, regional and ethnic materials, and more.*

Strategic Marketing in Library and Information Science, edited by Irene Owens (No. 28, 2002). *"A useful overview of marketing for LIS practitioners in a number of settings, including archives, public libraries, and LIS schools." (Barbara B. Moran, PhD, Professor, School of Information and Library Science, University of North Carolina-Chapel Hill)*

Out-of-Print and Special Collection Materials: Acquisition and Purchasing Options, edited by Judith Overmier (No. 27, 2002). *"Offers inspiration and advice to everyone who works with a special collection. Other librarians and bibliophiles who read it will come away with a new appreciation of the challenges and achievements of special collections librarians. . . . Also valuable for teachers who address these aspects of library work." (Peter Barker, PhD, Professor of the History of Science, University of Oklahoma, Norman)*

Publishing and the Law: Current Legal Issues, edited by A. Bruce Strauch (No. 26, 2001). Publishing and the Law: Current Legal Issues *provides lawyers and librarians with insight into the main areas of legal change that are having an impact on the scholarly publishing world today. This book explores constitutional issues, such as the Communications Decency Act, showing how the First Amendment makes it virtually impossible to regulate the World Wide Web. This unique book includes a history of copyright law up through current international treaties to provide an understanding of how copyright law and the electronic environment intertwine.*

Readers, Reading and Librarians, edited by Bill Katz (No. 25, 2001). *Reaffirms the enthusiasm of books and readers as libraries evolve from reading centers to information centers where librarians are now also web masters, information scientists, and media experts.*

Acquiring Online Management Reports, edited by William E. Jarvis (No. 24, 2000). *This fact-filled guide explores a broad variety of issues involving acquisitions and online management reports to keep libraries and library managers current with changing technology and, ultimately, offer patrons more information. This book provides you with discussions and suggestions on several topics, including working with vendors, developing cost-effective collection development methods to suit your library, assessing collection growth, and choosing the best electronic resources to help meet your goals.* Acquiring Online Management Reports *offers you an array of proven ideas, options, and examples that will enable your library to keep up with client demands and simplify the process of collecting, maintaining, and interpreting online reports.*

The Internet and Acquisitions: Sources and Resources for Development, edited by Mary E. Timmons (No. 23, 2000). *"For those trying to determine how the Internet could be of use to their particular library in the area of acquisitions, or for those who have already decided they should be moving in that direction . . . this volume is a good place to begin." (James Mitchell, MLS, Library Director, Bainbridge-Guilford Central School, Bainbridge, NY)*

Gifts and Exchanges: Problems, Frustrations, . . . and Triumphs, edited by Catherine Denning (No. 22, 1999). *"A complete compendium embracing all aspects of the matter in articles that are uniformly well-written by people experienced in this field." (Jonathan S. Tryon, CAL, JD, Professor, Graduate School of Library and Information Studies, University of Rhode Island)*

Periodical Acquisitions and the Internet, edited by Nancy Slight-Gibney (No. 21, 1999). *Sheds light on the emerging trends in selection, acquisition, and access to electronic journals.*

Public Library Collection Development in the Information Age, edited by Annabel K. Stephens (No. 20, 1998). *"A first-rate collection of articles . . . This is an engaging and helpful work for anyone involved in developing public library collections." (Lyn Hopper, MLn, Director, Chestatee Regional Library, Dahlonega, GA)*

Fiction Acquisition/Fiction Management: Education and Training, edited by Georgine N. Olson (No. 19, 1998). *"It is about time that attention is given to the collection in public libraries . . . it is about time that public librarians be encouraged to treat recreational reading with the same respect that is paid to informational reading . . . Thank you to Georgine Olson for putting this volume together." (Regan Robinson, MLS, Editor and Publisher, Librarian Collection Letter)*

Acquisitions and Collection Development in the Humanities, edited by Irene Owens (No. 17/18, 1997). *"Can easily become a personal reference tool." (William D. Cunningham, PhD, Retired faculty, College of Library and Information Service, University of Maryland, College Park)*

Approval Plans: Issues and Innovations, edited by John H. Sandy (No. 16, 1996). *"This book is valuable for several reasons, the primary one being that librarians in one-person libraries need to know how approval plans work before they can try one for their particular library . . . An important addition to the professional literature." (The One-Person Library)*

Current Legal Issues in Publishing, edited by A. Bruce Strauch (No. 15, 1996). *"Provides valuable access to a great deal of information about the current state of copyright thinking." (Library Association Record)*

New Automation Technology for Acquisitions and Collection Development, edited by Rosann Bazirjian (No. 13/14, 1995). *"Rosann Bazirjian has gathered together 13 current practitioners who explore technology and automation in acquisitions and collection development . . . Contains something for everyone." (Library Acquisitions: Practice and Theory)*

Management and Organization of the Acquisitions Department, edited by Twyla Racz and Rosina Tammany (No. 12, 1994). *"Brings together topics and librarians from across the country to discuss some basic challenges and changes facing our profession today." (Library Acquisitions: Practice and Theory)*

A. V. in Public and School Libraries: Selection and Policy Issues, edited by Margaret J. Hughes and Bill Katz (No. 11, 1994). *"Many points of view are brought forward for those who are creating new policy or procedural documents . . . Provide[s] firsthand experience as well as considerable background knowledge. . . ." (Australian Library Review)*

Multicultural Acquisitions, edited by Karen Parrish and Bill Katz (No. 9/10, 1993). *"A stimulating overview of the U.S. multicultural librarianship scene." (The Library Assn. Reviews)*

Popular Culture and Acquisitions, edited by Allen Ellis (No. 8, 1993). *"A provocative penetrating set of chapters on the tricky topic of popular culture acquisitions . . . A valuable guidebook." (Journal of Popular Culture)*

Collection Assessment: A Look at the RLG Conspectus©, edited by Richard J. Wood and Katina Strauch (No. 7, 1992). *"A well-organized, thorough book . . . Provides the most realistic representations of what the Conspectus is and what its limitations are . . . Will take an important place in Conspectus literature." (Library Acquisitions: Practice & Theory)*

Evaluating Acquisitions and Collections Management, edited by Pamela S. Cenzer and Cynthia I. Gozzi (No. 6, 1991). *"With the current emphasis on evaluation and return on funding, the material is timely indeed!" (Library Acquisitions: Practice & Theory)*

Vendors and Library Acquisitions, edited by Bill Katz (No. 5, 1991). *"Should be required reading for all new acquisitions librarians and all library science students who plan a career in technical services. As a whole it is a very valuable resource." (Library Acquisitions: Practice & Theory)*

Operational Costs in Acquisitions, edited by James R. Coffey (No. 4, 1991). *"For anyone interested in embarking on a cost study of the acquisitions process this book will be worthwhile reading." (Library Acquisitions: Practice & Theory)*

Legal and Ethical Issues in Acquisitions, edited by Katina Strauch and A. Bruce Strauch (No. 3, 1990). *"This excellent compilation is recommended to both collection development/acquisition librarians and library administrators in academic libraries." (The Journal of Academic Librarianship)*

The Acquisitions Budget, edited by Bill Katz (No. 2, 1989). *"Practical advice and tips are offered throughout . . . Those new to acquisitions work, especially in academic libraries, will find the book useful background reading." (Library Association Record)*

Automated Acquisitions: Issues for the Present and Future, edited by Amy Dykeman (No. 1, 1989). *"This book should help librarians to learn from the experience of colleagues in choosing the system that best suits their local requirements . . . [It] will appeal to library managers as well as to library school faculty and students." (Library Association Record)*

Managing Digital Resources in Libraries

Audrey Fenner
Editor

Managing Digital Resources in Libraries has been co-published simultaneously as *The Acquisitions Librarian*, Numbers 33/34 2005.

The Haworth Information Press®
An Imprint of The Haworth Press, Inc.

New York • London • Victoria (AU)
www.HaworthPress.com

Published by

The Haworth Information Press®, 10 Alice Street, Binghamton, NY 13904-1580 USA

The Haworth Information Press® is an imprint of The Haworth Press, Inc., 10 Alice Street, Binghamton, NY 13904-1580 USA.

Managing Digital Resources in Libraries has been co-published simultaneously as *The Acquisitions Librarian*, Numbers 33/34 2005.

Cover design by Lora Wiggins.

Library of Congress Cataloging-in-Publication Data

Managing digitial resources in libraries / Audrey Fenner, editor.
     p. cm.
     "Co-published simultaneously as The acquisitions librarian, numbers 33/34 2005."
     Includes bibliographical references and index.
     ISBN 0-7890-2402-0 (alk. paper) – ISBN 0-7890-2403-9 (pbk. : alk. paper)
     1. Digital libraries. 2. Libraries–Special collections–Electronic information resources. 3. Electronic information resources. 4. Libraries–Special collections–Electronic journals. 5. Electronic journals. 6. Libraries and electronic publishing. 7. Copyright–Electronic information resources–United States. 8. License agreements. 9. Digital libraries–Case studies. I. Fenner, Audrey. II. Acquisitions librarian.
    ZA4080.5 .M36 2004
    025'.00285–dc22
                                                    2004016751

Indexing, Abstracting & Website/Internet Coverage

This section provides you with a list of major indexing & abstracting services and other tools for bibliographic access. That is to say, each service began covering this periodical during the year noted in the right column. Most Websites which are listed below have indicated that they will either post, disseminate, compile, archive, cite or alert their own Website users with research-based content from this work. (This list is as current as the copyright date of this publication.)

(continued)

(continued)

Special Bibliographic Notes related to special journal issues (separates) and indexing/abstracting:

- indexing/abstracting services in this list will also cover material in any "separate" that is co-published simultaneously with Haworth's special thematic journal issue or DocuSerial. Indexing/abstracting usually covers material at the article/chapter level.
- monographic co-editions are intended for either non-subscribers or libraries which intend to purchase a second copy for their circulating collections.
- monographic co-editions are reported to all jobbers/wholesalers/approval plans. The source journal is listed as the "series" to assist the prevention of duplicate purchasing in the same manner utilized for books-in-series.
- to facilitate user/access services all indexing/abstracting services are encouraged to utilize the co-indexing entry note indicated at the bottom of the first page of each article/chapter/contribution.
- this is intended to assist a library user of any reference tool (whether print, electronic, online, or CD-ROM) to locate the monographic version if the library has purchased this version but not a subscription to the source journal.
- individual articles/chapters in any Haworth publication are also available through the Haworth Document Delivery Service (HDDS).

IN MEMORIAM

Dr. William (Bill) Katz passed away on September 12, 2004. Dr. Katz was Editor of the Haworth journals *The Acquisitions Librarian* and *The Reference Librarian* as well as *Magazines for Libraries, RQ* (the journal of the Reference and Adult Services Division of the American Library Association), and the "Magazines" column in *Library Journal.* In addition to his contributions to library science as an author and editor, he was a much-beloved professor in the School of Information Science and Policy at the State University of New York at Albany and a mentor to many of his former students in their professional lives. His association with The Haworth Press began in 1980 and lasted more than two decades. His steady hand, friendly guidance, and steadfast leadership will be missed by all of us at *The Acquisitions Librarian, The Reference Librarian,* and The Haworth Press.

Managing
Digital Resources
in Libraries

CONTENTS

ABOUT THE EDITOR

Audrey Fenner, MLS, BMus, BMusEd, ARCT, is Head, Acquisition Department at Walter Clinton Jackson Library, University of North Carolina at Greensboro. A librarian since 1984, Ms. Fenner has held professional positions in academic, research, business, government, and public libraries in the United States and Canada. She has had experience in a wide variety of library settings, from a one-person branch library housed in a trailer in the Arizona desert, to the National Library of Canada, where she did both original cataloging and reference work in two languages. Ms. Fenner holds a Master of Library Science degree from the University of Western Ontario, London, Canada.

Introduction:
Managing Digital Resources

Not many years ago, most libraries' acquisitions were limited to books, serials, microforms, and audiovisual materials. Today library patrons expect access to virtual documents as well as to physical items, and the concept of a library "collection" is being redefined. Leased electronic resources are made available to patrons without being acquired for the library. Intangible resources, such as the full text of articles, are provided through "pay per view" arrangements, and are used or taken away by patrons without ever being added to the library's permanent collection. It is becoming common for librarians to consider freely available Web resources as components of a collection, whether these resources are cataloged and appear in the OPAC, or are accessible through links on a library Web page. Attention is being paid to digitizing materials and publishing digital collections on the World Wide Web as a strategy to increase user access. A "collection" commonly extends beyond resources the library owns to include all the resources to which it can provide access.

The nature of publishing is changing. Publishers are moving away from the print model, which is expensive to deliver, in favor of electronic formats. This change gives rise to many questions. Textual content of e-journals and e-books is presented in such a way that it resembles hard copy print, much as automobiles in the early days of that industry were designed to look like horse-drawn conveyances. If electronic formats become the standard in publishing rather than hard copy print, how much sense will it make to ask readers to visualize a finite,

[Haworth co-indexing entry note]: "Introduction: Managing Digital Resources." Fenner, Audrey. Co-published simultaneously in *The Acquisitions Librarian* (The Haworth Information Press, an imprint of The Haworth Press, Inc.) No. 33/34, 2005, pp. 1-5; and: *Managing Digital Resources in Libraries* (ed: Audrey Fenner) The Haworth Information Press, an imprint of The Haworth Press, Inc., 2005, pp. 1-5. Single or multiple copies of this article are available for a fee from The Haworth Document Delivery Service [1-800-HAWORTH, 9:00 a.m. - 5:00 p.m. (EST). E-mail address: docdelivery@haworthpress.com].

Digital Object Identifier: 10.1300/J101v17n33_01

book-like object, or a single issue of a serial, when they want access to information?

Where does the content of one issue of an electronic journal or one e-book leave off and another begin, when we are considering data transmitted by electrical impulses rather than markings on a page? The intellectual content of digital resources exists not on paper but in a nonmaterial state, as an entity the user envisions but which has no corresponding physical reality. Has printed text been transformed into a philosophical abstraction?

Publishers are experimenting with various pricing and delivery models, just as librarians are trying various ways of incorporating electronic publications into their selection, acquisition and cataloging routines. Publishers offer idiosyncratic approaches for acquisitions librarians to consider, such as books that combine print text with electronic, Web-based text or bibliographies. Catalogers have the option of using new metadata standards that provide for the inclusion of tables of contents and book reviews in the OPAC. Electronic formats have changed the focus of serials work without fully displacing the print medium. Hard copy and electronic versions of scholarly journals serve different purposes: readers may prefer hard copy for photos and graphics, while electronic versions are easier to use in searching citations. Results of scholarly research may be disseminated through the Web without being published at all, and reach at least as wide an audience as printed articles that have gone through a formal peer review process.

How are librarians coping with digital resources? How do they compare and select titles and formats to purchase? How do they allocate limited funds, to lease or purchase high-priced electronic titles? Does consortium membership provide the answer to funding problems, or does it force librarians to pay for content their users neither want nor need? Are librarians able to make themselves familiar with the multitude of resources available? Questions like these are considered in the articles that follow.

LICENSING

Concerns with licensing electronic products are discussed by contributors to this volume. Min Chou and Oliver Zhou examine the licensing of digital resources and the effect this has had on collection management. Rather than positing the now-common dichotomy between ownership and access, the authors claim that "restrictions imposed by licensing agreements have turned the library's collection into two parts: owned and leased." They make the assertion that "this new intellectual legal framework rewards those who make information inaccessible." Chou and Zhou describe the legal mechanism established by the Digital Millennium Copyright Act, the nature and types of licensing agreements for electronic products, and the legal philosophy that underlies them. They state that digital content providers and libraries have differing values, and those differences are interfering with libraries' efforts to achieve their mission. They conclude that libraries must promote the First Sale Doctrine and the Fair Use Doctrine in the digital environment.

Timothy Shipe's article on the licensing of electronic products uses a fictional scenario to illustrate the many barriers and frustrations librarians encounter in reviewing licenses. Shipe writes from his experience as a humanities bibliographer who is the person responsible for reviewing and negotiating all licenses for the library where he works.

OPINIONS, RESEARCH, AND ANALYSIS

Eugenio Pelizzari provides an account of sweeping changes to the scholarly communication paradigm. He provides a history of the Open Archives movement, and a state-of-the-art account of its feasibility in the face of technical barriers and limited acceptance. If an e-print archive existed, compliant with an accepted OAI standard, Pelizzari offers reasons why it would provide a complement to traditional means of scholarly communication and publishing.

In a study of advertisements for library positions, Emerita Cuesta provides good insights into the ways positions are, or are not, being reconfigured. Using ads with position titles like "electronic services librarian" or "digital services librarian," Cuesta discerns trends in assigning responsibilities for managing digital materials.

An article by Donna Skekel describes how the library of a small liberal arts college is adding online resources to its collection. Skekel discusses the methods and technology used, and whether libraries are able to fulfill the original "library mission statement" proposed by Charles Cutter in his *Rules for a Dictionary Catalog*. Skekel raises several timely questions: how to provide article-level access to journals, the effect on collection management of purchasing aggregations of journals, and whether MARC is still an appropriate format for cataloging.

SYSTEMS AND SOFTWARE

Librarians have adopted various means of providing access to electronic journals. Cataloging e-journals provides an obvious solution to the question of access, and results in a truly integrated collection of journals in all formats. Cecilia Leathem describes approaches that can be taken to cataloging electronic journals, and offers a clear, comprehensible summary of the advantages and disadvantages of each option.

Another solution to the problem of providing access to electronic journals is the use of e-journal management software. Anna Alwerud and Lotte Jorgensen describe "ELIN@," a management system for e-journals developed at Lund University Libraries in Sweden. ELIN@ offers article-level searching of e-journals, makes other electronic materials searchable, allows easy ordering, and provides statistics for administrative analysis. The system is used by ten academic libraries in Sweden.

Randle Gedeon and George Boston of Western Michigan University provide an account of Waldo Library's TDNet installation, called "Electronic Journal Finder." The writers describe the implementation of the system, its positive aspects, and some limitations for searching.

Clark Nall and Janice Steed Lewis describe the development of "Pirate Source" at East Carolina University's Joyner Library. This is a dynamic, database-driven Web site, developed in-house, that provides library users with access to resources of all types. It functions as a starting point for research and also serves instructional purposes.

Sue Anderson, writing from Eastern Washington University, describes that library's two-part solution to providing access to the content of full-text aggregators and collections. Digital materials can be searched in the OPAC and also in a Cold Fusion database available on the library's Web site.

SPECIAL PROJECTS AND HISTORIES

Denise Koufogiannakis, Pam Ryan and Susan Dahl describe the successful integration of PDA-accessible resources into the collection of the University of Alberta Libraries. This project began with health sciences titles available on the Internet and expanded to include purchased, licensed resources. At these libraries, PDA-accessible titles are regarded as one more format among many. Making them available to library users has brought about novel solutions to questions of licensing, cataloging, processing and storing these non-standard materials.

Harvey Brenneise presents topics of concern in developing an all-digital public health library, the Michigan Community Health Electronic Library. He discusses cataloging questions, concerns with digitizing special and unique collections, and collaborative ventures with other health libraries in Michigan.

Judith Hiott and Carla Beasley compare the purchase and management of electronic resources in two public libraries, one a multi-branch system in a large metropolitan area, the other a somewhat smaller but growing county system with two branches. The authors discuss changes in the collection and management of resources as budgets for print and digital resources were merged. They describe a pattern that manifested itself over a period of time: adding electronic resources, weeding them as funding declined, then stabilizing both budgets and collections.

Audrey Fenner

LICENSING

The Impact of Licenses on Library Collections

Min Chou
Oliver Zhou

SUMMARY. The increasing popularity of digital information has brought great convenience to library patrons. It has, however, posed challenges to libraries in achieving their major missions, i.e., preservation and dissemination of information. The underlying reasons for this phenomenon are dichotomous: the restrictions imposed by electronic information licensing agreements and unreliability of digital content. During the transition from a traditional library to a digital one, libraries spend more to

Min Chou is Reference Librarian, Congressman Frank J. Guarini Library, New Jersey City University, 2039 Kennedy Boulevard, Jersey City, NJ 07305-1597 (E-mail: mchou@njcu.edu). Oliver Zhou is a practicing attorney, Law Offices of Oliver Zhou, 350 Broadway, Suite 406, New York, NY 10013 (E-mail: ozhou@aol.com). He is a member of New York and New Jersey Bars, and has been admitted to practice at the U.S. Supreme Court, the U.S. Court of Appeals for the Second Circuit, and the U.S. Court of International Trade.

[Haworth co-indexing entry note]: "The Impact of Licenses on Library Collections." Chou, Min, and Oliver Zhou. Co-published simultaneously in *The Acquisitions Librarian* (The Haworth Information Press, an imprint of The Haworth Press, Inc.) No. 33/34, 2005, pp. 7-23; and: *Managing Digital Resources in Libraries* (ed: Audrey Fenner) The Haworth Information Press, an imprint of The Haworth Press, Inc., 2005, pp. 7-23. Single or multiple copies of this article are available for a fee from The Haworth Document Delivery Service [1-800-HAWORTH, 9:00 a.m. - 5:00 p.m. (EST). E-mail address: docdelivery@haworthpress.com].

acquire both print and digital resources simultaneously. This dual format mode puts more pressure upon libraries' shrinking acquisition budget. Digital content providers have turned the digital content from sale to lease through licensing, and the licensing terms usually restrict libraries in delivering effective and efficient virtual library services to users. For the collective good of society, the only real solution will be the digital First Sale Doctrine established for library exemption. *[Article copies available for a fee from The Haworth Document Delivery Service: 1-800-HAWORTH. E-mail address: <docdelivery@haworthpress.com> Website: <http://www.HaworthPress.com> © 2005 by The Haworth Press, Inc. All rights reserved.]*

KEYWORDS. Academic libraries, collection development, license agreements, copyright, electronic information resources, online databases, license agreements–law and legislation–United States

Throughout history, libraries have always acted and functioned as information repositories and disseminators. Libraries, especially academic libraries, play a central role in promoting the progress of science and arts. This role, however, is under serious attack by the commercialization of digital content brought by the Internet revolution. One hallmark of this commercialization of digital content is the popularity of licensing agreements in the current marketplace, including both mass-market licensing agreements and negotiated licensing agreements. Licensing agreements are essentially a type of private legislation launched by digital content developers who believe that the U.S. copyright law has not provided adequate protection for their intellectual property rights. Under the context of a typical licensing agreement, libraries pay for the use of the digital content under the various restrictions imposed by a digital content provider. Libraries no longer own the physical copy of the digital content, nor do they have the physical custody of digital contents and the software system, notwithstanding the fact that they pay hefty fees for subscribing to them.

This phenomenon is largely due to the fact that libraries have increasingly relied upon digital resources as opposed to print material, as a result of the emerging popularity of e-commerce, and the convenience that digital technology has brought to the business operation of libraries. However, the 1998 Digital Millennium Copyright Act (DMCA) has set up a legal mechanism of anti-circumvention measures, which has made it illegal to bypass any anti-circumvention measure, such as an encryption code or other kind of digital fences, designed by copyright owners to control access to their works (17 U.S.C. §1201). This anti-circumvention provision guarantees the right of digital content providers to control access to their copyrighted works by imposing any restrictive terms as they see fit upon users as to the time, place, and manner of information use. In other words, digital content providers can regulate how end users can use their software system and the digital content, and under what condition and for what purposes.

The passage of the DMCA and the wide use of licensing agreements have essentially done away with the First Sale Doctrine in a digital environment. This development has seriously undermined the library's role as an information repository on the one hand and disseminator on the other. As a result, libraries have been forced to face a daunting uphill battle to achieve their mission to preserve and to disseminate information for the advancement of science and arts. Libraries are forced to embark upon a journey of fighting for their survival.

This paper first discusses the new digital legal mechanism established by the DMCA and its anti-circumvention provision. It then delineates the nature of licensing agreements and further defines those agreements. It moves on to discuss the types of licensing agreements and the underlying legal philosophy. The fourth part discusses the differences in core values between digital content providers and libraries, and their enduring conflicts in pursuit of their missions. The fifth part discusses the impact of licensing agreements upon libraries' acquisitions and collections. The sixth part suggests strategies and proposes objectives in negotiating licensing agreements. Finally, the paper concludes that libraries should promote the First Sale Doctrine and the Fair Use Doctrine in the digital environment. Only then can libraries achieve their missions successfully.

I. THE CURRENT LEGAL SYSTEM OF COPYRIGHT PROTECTION

The current American copyright legal system is mainly constituted by a three-layered protection, i.e., the 1976 Copyright Act, the 1998 Digital Millennium Copyright Act, and the state contract law and various case laws. Section 109(a) of the 1976 Copyright Act establishes the First Sale Doctrine, under which a buyer of copyrighted works can lend, resell, and dispose of them without the copyright holders' consent (17 U.S.C. §109). Section 107 of the Copyright Act sets forth the Fair Use Doctrine, under which the reproduction of copyrighted materials does not constitute an act of copyright infringement so long as it is for the purposes of fair use such as criticism, comment, news reporting, teaching, scholarship, or research (17 U.S.C. §107). To determine whether a use of copyrighted work is fair use, American courts usually employ a four-factor analysis as follows: first, the purpose and character of the use, including whether such use is of commercial nature or is for nonprofit educational purposes; second, the nature of the copyrighted work; third, the amount and substantiality of the portion used in relation to the copyrighted work as a whole; and fourth, the effect of the use upon the potential fair market value of the copyrighted work (Chou and Zhou "Academic," 312-313).

The First Sale Doctrine and the Fair Use Doctrine have long been the two pillars that guarantee the operation of modern libraries. Without these two doctrines, libraries could not legally operate to function as information repositories and to disseminate information to their constituents. Fairly speaking, the 1976 Copyright Act has served both our society and copyright owners very well in terms of promoting the advancement of science and arts and rewarding the creativeness of authors and copyright owners.

The DMCA has changed the delicate balance between societal interests and copyright owners' benefit. Section 1201(a)(1)(A) of the DMCA provides that "no person shall circumvent a technological measure that effectively controls access to a work protected under this title" (17 U.S.C. §1201). It makes it illegal to access copyrighted works that are protected by technological measures, such as password, encryption, or even remote disabling devices embedded in the software system. This anti-circumvention provision guarantees the right of digital content providers to control access to their copyrighted works. It further opens the gate for digital content providers to impose any restrictive terms they see fit upon users as to the time, place, and manner of use of their products. In other words, digital content providers can regulate how end users can use their software system and the digital content, and under what condition and for what purposes.

II. DEFINING LICENSING AGREEMENTS

1. The Nature of Licensing Agreements

The explosive developments of new digital technologies in the past decade have made it possible for digital content providers to develop electronic contents at an unprecedented pace. It is true that a vast amount of information is available free of charge on the World Wide Web. Much information, however, is copyrighted and owned by digital content providers. To access the copyrighted content, permissions or licenses are required from digital content providers. At present, libraries need licenses to access a variety of digital resources including, but not limited to, the following: (1) an online subscription to a journal or database; (2) content compiled by an aggregator such as LexisNexis; (3) an encyclopedia or other collections of content; (4) financial information, stock market sources, and news feeds; (5) computer software, CD-ROMs, and DVDs; (6) preexisting content for use on Web site or Intranet, including text, graphic content, such as maps and photographs, music, and video; (7) Web site content; and (8) Intranet content (Harris 2).

Licensing agreements, as stated by Easterbrook, one of the most influential circuit judges in the United States, are "ordinary contracts accompanying the sale of products, and therefore as governed by the common law of contracts and the Uniform Commercial Code" (ProCD v. Zeidenberg, 1447). Most materials libraries acquired are copyrighted works. "Normally, to use a copyrighted work, one must obtain from the copyright owner a license whose terms are determined by or through private bargaining" (Joyce et al., 492). The terms of licenses depend on the prevailing market conditions at a given time and the bargaining power of the parties. Therefore, licenses essentially regulate the business relationship between the parties.

2. Types of Licensing Agreements

There are a number of different categories of licensing agreements. The first one is a statutory or compulsory license. Under a statutory license, a third party such as a library can use a copyrighted work without the copyright owner's permission, so long as the party complies with the legal requirements and pays royalties. There are currently six compulsory licenses recognized by the United States copyright law such as the Digital Performance Right in Sound Recording, etc. (Joyce et al., 493). In this instance, the copyright law obviously takes precedence over the normal market mechanism for negotiating a licensing agreement.

The second type of licensing agreements is so-called "shrink-wrap" licenses. A shrink-wrap license is a form agreement packaged with consumer software products. A consumer agrees to be bound by the terms of a shrink-wrap license by virtue of his opening the software package.

A shrink-wrap license is also called a "click-on" license. In click-on licenses, a consumer accepts the terms of the license by clicking an "I Accept" button on the computer screen at a time when he/she is installing the software. Shrink-wrap licenses have recently become a mass-market tool in the United States.

The third type of license is negotiable licensing agreements. Under this type of license, contract parties discuss and agree upon the terms and conditions acceptable to both parties. As an institutional consumer, a library will have good chances to encounter this type of licensing agreement during its course of procurement of digital content, as the number of electronic resources has been growing explosively. Unlike an individual consumer, institutional patrons such as academic libraries generally have much better bargaining power to negotiate favorable terms and conditions suited to their needs.

III. WHY LICENSING AGREEMENTS EXIST

1. Different Types of Legal Protection Modes

A. Copyright Law Protection

There are a number of legal mechanisms currently in place protecting computer software, i.e., patent law, copyright law, trade secret law, and state contract law. Of those protection mechanisms, copyright law provides the most important legal umbrella for computer software and digital content. Copyright law protects original works of authorship. American courts have consistently held that originality is the touchstone of copyright protection (Feist Publications, Inc. v. Rural Telephone Service Company, Inc.). Section 102 of U.S. copyright law protects the literary, musical, graphic, or artistic form in which authors expressed intellectual concepts (17 U.S.C. §102). Computer software is the form of expression created by a programmer, therefore, it can be categorized as a literary work, and can be copyrighted (Apple Computer, Inc. v. Franklin Computer Corp.).

B. Patent Law Protection

Copyright law, however, does not protect the actual processes or methods embodied in the program (17 U.S.C. 102(b)). Many software developers believe that the protection of computer software provided by copyright law is inadequate. They look for other alternative modes of protection such as patent. They achieved great success in protecting software under patent law in 1981 when the U.S. Supreme Court upheld the patentability of a software-related invention in Diamond v. Diehr. The biggest advantage of patent law protection of computer software is that patent law guards against independent creation of software programs since patents require novelty, utility and nonobviousness. However, the patent law has drawbacks as well. First, patent application is expensive and time-consuming. It takes about two years to get it and incurs large sums in legal fees since the patent standard of novelty, utility, and nonobviousness is strict in a legal sense. Typically, the software life span is only a couple of years. Second, patent application requires disclosure of key elements of the program. The disclosure of source codes of software divulges any trade secret protection the software developers would otherwise enjoy.

C. Trade Secret Law Protection

A trade secret may well be protected so long as it is kept secret by enforcing the confidentiality clause in the franchise licensing agreement. Any improper disclosure of trade secrets can be enjoined based on the tort theory of conversion (Joyce, 175). The drawback of trade secret protection is that it is vulnerable to reverse engineering. Therefore, software developers have turned to a more effective protection mode, i.e., licensing agreements under state contract law or UCC.

2. Underlying Legal Philosophy Behind Licensing Agreements

According to Circuit Judge Easterbrook, "A copyright is a right against the world" (ProCD v. Zeidenberg, 1454). Contracts, by contrast, generally affect only their parties; strangers may do as they please, so contracts do not create "exclusive rights" (ProCD v. Zeidenberg, 1454). Despite the drawbacks of contract law, contracts or licenses have proven to be a powerful legal tool to protect the interests of software developers or digital content providers no matter whether the software is custom designed or a mass-market product. The popularity of licensing agreements as a business operation model is the direct result of "private legislation" of copyright-type rights initiated by software developers (Chou and Zhou "Examining," 48). Software developers believe that statutory copyright law and patent law do not provide adequate protection against pirates due to the nature of the software, since it is easily copied and distributed. More importantly, the software industry has imitated the business operation model of public utility companies to turn software sales into licenses or leases by charging customers a fee for use on a regular basis, thereby generating a continuous stream of income. To achieve this goal, they launched relentless assaults on two fronts. On the one hand, they lobbied Congress successfully to eliminate the First Sale Doctrine in the digital world, as evidenced by the passage of DMCA in 1998. On the other hand, they inserted very restrictive licensing terms into their software packages, and forced consumers to accept the terms and conditions unilaterally imposed by them without being aware of the fact that it is software licensing rather than software sale, notwithstanding the consumer understanding that it is the sale of software. This type of license is labeled as "shrink-wrap licensing agreements" since the retail software packages are covered in plastic cellophane shrink-wrap (Chou and Zhou "Examining," 48). The "click-on license" is of the same nature. Digital content providers assume that consumers consent to the terms of the license by merely clicking on the screen button "I Accept" or by opening the software package.

As a matter of fact, this type of licensing agreement is, by nature, the contract of adhesion. Consumers must either take it or leave it, for there is no negotiation conducted between a digital content provider and a consumer. Without exception, licensing agreements comprise favorable and lengthy terms to digital content providers or software developers. The majority of consumers lack the necessary information, time and training to fully comprehend the legal and technical terms of the licensing agreements. These factual circumstances have led to a big intellectual debate among legal professionals in the United States, European Union and other continents regarding the legality of these licensing agreements (Determann and Fellmeth).

There are divergent trends running in opposite directions in American case law with regard to the legality and enforceability of licensing agreements. One school advocated the enforceability of licensing agreements, and 7th Circuit Judge Easterbrook is the one who is carrying the red banner. On the other end of the legal spectrum, the U.S. Third Circuit and a number of other courts declared that shrink-wrap or click-on licensing agreements are legally unenforceable because they violated public policy in the United States (Step-Saver Data Sys. Inc. v. Wyse Technology). ProCD v. Zeidenberg is a very powerful opinion written by one of the most influential judges in the United States. It is, however, widely criticized by professional critics for its failure to protect consumer interests (Schechter, 1758). The passage of the DMCA and the growing acceptance of the legitimacy of licensing agreements by American courts, along with the looming Uniform Computer Information Transactions Act (UCITA) have marked the coming of a new era for libraries. This new digital era is characterized by clashes between libraries and digital content providers, due to the significant difference in fundamental values between these two social institutions.

IV. VALUE CONFLICTS BETWEEN ACADEMIC LIBRARIES AND DIGITAL CONTENT PROVIDERS

According to Professor Laura Gasaway, the primary values of libraries and digital content providers relating to copyright law are many. The core values of authors and publishers relating to copyright include: (1) compensation for the creation and production of their works, (2) ability to control their works, (3) authentication and recognition of their works, (4) broad marketing of their works, (5) promoting strong intellectual property rights, and (6) viewing the fair use doctrine as an affirmative defense to copyright infringement. Libraries' core values regarding copyright law include: (1) recognition of public libraries as educational institutions, (2) providing information to the people, (3) providing information on all sides of an issue, (4) promoting the rights of users of copyrighted works, (5) ability to identify and locate information, (6) recognition of the importance of the public domain as a repository of information, and (7) viewing the Fair Use Doctrine as a right of a person to use a copyrighted work. The collective good of society shared by libraries, publishers, and producers relating to copyright includes: (1) the importance of an educated population, (2) the support of entrepreneurship, (3) access to public libraries, (4) the importance of the public domain, and (5) public access to information (Gasaway, 116-117).

This list of core values related to copyright indicates that there are major differences between these two groups with regard to their fundamental values. The differences in values determine the different approaches between these two groups in achieving and promoting their missions. Digital content providers generally favor a pay-per-use distribution system based on licensing agreements. Libraries need a digital First Sale Doctrine and digital Fair Use Doctrine to support research and teaching activities, and to promote public access to information and preservation of information. Those differences have inevitably led to a confrontation between the two groups in both business and legal battlegrounds. In shaping the new digital world order of intellectual property law, digital content providers, armed with plenty of money, have aggressively lobbied the U.S. Congress to legislate many new laws to protect their interests. Their values have prevailed over those of libraries. The legal landscape in the digital environment in the past decade indicated that the scale has been decisively tipped towards digital content providers rather than libraries. The simple fact of the matter is that libraries have been essentially marginalized in their course of promoting their values and achieving their mission.

First and foremost, DMCA failed to provide library use and exemption privileges to ensure libraries' operation in the digital environment. DMCA is the U.S. domestic implementation of the World Intellectual Property Organization (WIPO) Copyright Treaty, in which the United States is a member. The WIPO Copyright Treaty has adopted the following basic copyright rules in the digital environment: (1) Copyright owners should have an exclusive right to control the making of copies of their works in digital form. (2) They should have an exclusive right to control the communication of their works to the public. (3) Treaty countries can continue to apply existing exceptions and limitations, such as the Fair Use Doctrine, as appropriate to the digital environment, and can even create new exceptions and limitations appropriate to the digital environment. (4) Merely providing facilities for the communications of works should not be a basis for infringement liability. (5) It should be illegal to tamper with copyright management information insofar as this would facilitate or conceal infringement in the digital environment. (6) Countries should have adequate legal protection and effective legal remedies against the circumvention of effective technological measures used by copyright owners to protect their works from infringing uses (Chou and Zhou "Academic," 309-310).

In fact, the WIPO Copyright Treaty has left ample room for each individual member country to enact laws in the digital environment. There could be a chance for libraries to lobby Congress to pass laws establishing the Library Use Exemption, the First Sale Doctrine and Fair Use Doctrine in the digital environment. However, digital content providers took the center stage of the show and made the anti-circumvention measure the centerpiece of DMCA. Armed with this legal protection, digital content providers can embed any technical devices such as a remote disabler to maintain their absolute control of the digital content. This anti-circumvention clause has effectively ruled out the First Sale Doctrine, and left the Fair Use Doctrine at the mercy of digital content providers in the digital environment. This has not only given digital content providers an upper hand in controlling the distribution of electronic resources by the means of licensing agreements, but has also put the libraries in a very precarious position in promoting their values and achieving their missions.

Digital content providers have effectively used the powerful tool of the licensing agreements to turn the sale of electronic resources to the scheme of licenses or leases, which has enabled them to generate a steady stream of income by their mass-market shrink-wrap or click-on licenses without losing any control of any digital content. While libraries might still arguably have some bargaining power simply due to their sheer size and budget power, they now still have to fight an uphill battle to receive preset benefits negotiated with digital content providers in order to achieve their mission for public access to information and to promote the research and teaching activities.

V. THE IMPACT OF LICENSING AGREEMENTS UPON LIBRARY COLLECTIONS

The commitment to ongoing and enduring access to information has long been cherished as a core value of libraries, especially academic libraries, since libraries are generally recognized as stewards of cultural and intellectual heritage (Thomas, 104). Because of this ongoing and enduring commitment, preservation of the collection has become an integral part of the academic library's business operation. Traditionally, libraries have devoted a tremendous amount of their funding to purchase print collections and to preserve these tangible items, since they require large amounts of space and maintenance costs are high. Digital technologies, however, have begun to affect the acquisition practices of the library. The digital collection has technical superiority over the print collection because digital information is easy to use, copy, and distribute without degradation and decay. The biggest pitfall lies in the fact that digital information is leased under licensing agreements rather than being owned by libraries, even though they pay hefty subscription fees to digital content providers. The elimination of the First Sale Doctrine in the DMCA and the wide use of licensing agreements have made libraries lose physical custody of these collections, since libraries can no longer freely use, lend, and dispose of the digital collection as they see necessary to promote the progress of science and useful arts.

At present, many digital content providers publish resources in both digital and print formats. The attractiveness and technical superiority of digital technology have compelled libraries to acquire resources in digital format. However, the lack of physical custody, plus the uncertain nature of shifting technology and changing technical standards have made libraries uncomfortable with complete reliance upon a digital collection. According to Sarah Thomas, a librarian at Cornell University, one survey indicated that 84% of libraries surveyed would cancel print if perpetual access to digital content were reliable (Thomas, 105). This survey result indicates that librarians tend to view digital content providers as being unable to guarantee academic libraries perpetual access to digital contents. This view is certainly the reflection of the current reality shaped by licensing agreements.

Another survey conducted by Kevin M. Guthrie indicated another fact why academic libraries are locked into collecting dual formats (Guthrie, Slide 34). The survey found that nearly 78% of people expressed the view that "regardless of what happens with electronic journals, it will always be crucial for libraries to maintain hard copy archives" (Guthrie, Slide 28). There is also a consensus among various organizations such as the Council on Library and Information Resources, the Digital Library Federation, the Coalition for Networked Information, the National Science Foundation, the Society for Scholarly Publishing, and the Andrew W. Mellon Foundation that digital collection should be held in multiple locations to guarantee perpetual access to them. The underlying rationale for this belief is that the business operation of digital content providers may be affected by a variety of economic variables such as bankruptcy, acquisition and merger, and strategic alliance among different players in the field (Thomas, 105).

The dual format of library collections is also created by the legal mechanism of licensing agreements. Licensing agreements generally impose strict terms on libraries as to the time, place and manner of use of digital content. Those agreements eliminate the First Sale Doctrine and often restrict or even prohibit libraries from using licensed digital content in interlibrary loan (ILL), electronic reserve, electronic preservation, and virtual reference service. Many electronic resources even contain monitoring and remote disabling devices to observe how libraries use digital content, and whether the uses comply with the terms and conditions of the licensing agreements. These hidden devices could remotely disable the use of digital content or databases if any activities that do not conform to the terms of the licensing agreements are detected. However, the convenience of electronic resources and the desire of libraries to offer efficient services have induced libraries to keep building their digital collections. Thus, the legal mechanism of licensing agreements has put an onerous burden upon libraries in achieving their mission, and has severely restricted their ability to disseminate information and to promote the advancement of sciences and arts.

Many people may believe that development of digital collections will result in significant savings for libraries, since digital publishing will reduce the costs associated with editing, producing, storing, and distributing information. This presumption, however, is unfounded wishful thinking. As a matter of fact, the business operation model of digital content publishers is that they offer digital and print subscriptions for a "bundled" price, usually 10% to 30% higher than the price of the print subscription alone (JSTOR 1). This practice actually increases the cost of the subscription rather than reducing it.

Moreover, the pricing strategy of digital content providers most likely is not based on the actual costs of designing and manufacturing the digital content, but rather is based on the economic theory of whatever the market can bear (Meyer, 327; Alford, 634). Alternatively, digital content providers might also take the producing costs with a certain rate of profit margin into consideration in determining the price. Of these factors, we can be sure of one thing, that the cost is absolutely not the only factor in the pricing equation. Under most circumstances, digital content providers do not offer the same price tag for every database. Rather, they have different pricing packages for different users with different needs, such as flat-fee subscription or a pay-per-use subscription.

Libraries have been subject to increasing pressure to operate themselves more efficiently under tighter budgets. The rising costs of journal subscriptions have eaten up a large chunk of the library budget; subscription costs rise rapidly as a result of the fact that the number of journals has grown quickly, and most libraries are being asked to cut their budgets. By contrast, library patrons are demanding more with higher expectations than ever that libraries should make more information in digital format available so that patrons can access the information wherever they are and whenever they want. What is the solution for libraries to meet the challenge of this changing environment under the restraints of licensing agreements?

JSTOR believes that digital technology promises a clear solution. Its joint report "Preserving Digital Information" suggests that pooled resource sharing among libraries can help capture the savings even though it is not less expensive for a single library to do so (JSTOR 1). One commentator, however, pointed out that digital resources would not save money because savings from paper reproduction and distribution are offset by increased investments associated with digital technology (Miller, 97). Even JSTOR, a nonprofit organization created to serve libraries and their users, still imposes restrictive terms not favorable to libraries in its licensing agreement. Under JSTOR's licensing agreement, e-mail online document delivery is prohibited, and users are allowed to download an electronic copy of an article and print one copy only for their non-commercial use; library licensees do not have the ownership right to JSTOR's software to retrieve the items, nor are library licensees allowed to archive articles in JSTOR's electronic repository of scholarly journals (Alford, 634). Worse, JSTOR's products are sold "as is" without any warranty (Alford, 634). JSTOR further has the right to change the terms of the license or any aspect of the JSTOR database at any time without notice (Alford, 634). Such restrictive terms imposed by licensing agreements have made cost savings impossible, since they prevent libraries from effectively using and sharing digital content.

VI. STRATEGIES AND OBJECTIVES IN NEGOTIATING LICENSING AGREEMENTS

1. Strategies in Negotiating Licensing Agreements

A major issue facing academic libraries in their digital content acquisition is how the libraries can use digital resources in a varied environment. Many universities now have multiple locations. More and more universities have fast-growing distance education programs. Under this kind of academic setting, it is inevitable that academic libraries need to provide virtual library services to their users. Otherwise the services provided by an academic library would obviously not meet the demand of teaching and research activities.

Under the current three-layered legal landscape shaped by the Copyright Act, the DMCA, and licensing agreements, virtual library services such as online document delivery and electronic reserve have become a very tricky issue. The First Sale Doctrine does not apply to digital contents, and the Fair Use Doctrine has been severely restricted. Under this kind of circumstance, the best practice for academic libraries is to negotiate a favorable license with digital content providers allowing virtual library services to the faculty and students. One of the best strategies to achieve this objective is consortial acquisition. The buying power of a large group of libraries can provide the benefits of economy of scale to the member libraries, thereby bringing down the costs associated with acquiring digital resources. Secondly, consortial and other cooperative acquisition models can win more favorable licensing terms from digital content providers, such as certain types of interlibrary loan (ILL) activities and other virtual library services. As pointed out by John Webb, academic libraries have been getting better and better licensing terms from digital content providers as "librarians become more adept at negotiating and as publishers and vendors become more comfortable in removing or modifying counterproductive restrictions" (200). Some digital content providers, such as the American Chemical Society and Elsevier, allow interlibrary loan from Web issues, although this is still more restrictive than the fair use provision of section 107 of the Copyright Act allows (Webb, 201).

Consortial acquisition does not benefit academic libraries alone. It works for digital content providers as well, since it can increase their market share and reduce the costs of maintaining an ongoing business relationship with customers (Webb, 202, 203).

2. Objectives in Negotiating Licensing Agreements

Justice Sandra Day O'Connor wrote in one opinion that the primary objective of copyright is not to reward the labor of authors, but to promote the progress of science and useful arts (Feist Publications Inc. v. Rural Telephone Service Company, Inc., 349). The advancement of science and arts is the underlying collective good and is the moral interest of the copyright law (Chou, 28). One mandate of copyright is to promote the dissemination of culture and knowledge in society. However, the elimination of the First Sale Doctrine in the digital environment, and the eradication of the First Sale Doctrine by the anti-circumvention measure affirmed by DMCA, have run afoul of the most important underlying philosophy of copyright, i.e., the advancement of science and arts. This new intellectual legal framework rewards those who make information inaccessible. The wide use of licensing agreements and technological measures to build digital fences has disturbed the delicate balance between intellectual property protection and freedom of information (Hugenholtz, 86).

Given the fact that digital content acquisition costs hefty fees, academic libraries should negotiate licenses that confirm digital content transfers as sales rather than leases. Section 1201 (a)(1)(A) does not explicitly authorize copyright owners to impose technological restraints on the resale of copies of protected works, and section 109(a) requires a sale of content to include resale rights (17 U.S.C. §109, §1201). Therefore, academic libraries are able to provide online document delivery and other virtual library services legally. If digital content providers would embed remote disablers or other technical impediment devices to prevent academic libraries from offering virtual library services, and to terminate libraries' subscriptions, or start launching lawsuits against academic libraries for any action of infringement by virtue of the use of anti-circumvention measures, academic libraries could defend themselves with a claim of copyright misuse for any attempt by the copyright owners to extend their statutory monopoly power beyond the scope allowed by the 1976 Copyright Act (Determann and Fellmeth, 70).

Libraries can further defend their reproduction rights under the exemption granted by section 108 of Copyright Act (17 U.S.C. §108). Under section 108, a library can reproduce a work without incurring any potential legal liability so long as it satisfies the following three requirements: (1) there is no direct or indirect commercial advantage to the library, (2) the library must either be open to the public or to researchers doing research in the same or similar field, and (3) the reproduction must contain a notice of copyright (Chou and Zhou, 314).

With these two layers of legal protection, libraries are in a better position to apply the First Sale Doctrine to digital content. The firm establishment of the First Sale Doctrine in the digital environment could become a real, practical solution to solve the problem of the dual format acquisition mode caused by licensing agreements.

VII. CONCLUSION

The massive onslaught of licensing agreements upon library digital resource acquisition has severely interfered with the library's function of information repository and disseminator. Restrictions imposed by licensing agreements have divided the library's collection into two parts: owned and leased. This situation is not cost effective and service efficient. One practical way out of this situation is to transform the digital content license from lease to sale. Only the establishment of the First Sale Doctrine in the digital environment can alleviate the negative impact upon the library acquisition process imposed by unfair licensing agreements.

REFERENCES

Alford, Duncan E. "Negotiating and Analyzing Electronic License Agreements." *Law Library Journal* 94 (Fall 2002): 621-644.

Apple Computer, Inc. v. Franklin Computer Corp. 714 F.2d 1240. 3d Cir. Ct. 1983.

Chou, Min. "Ethics and Copyright Issues on Campus." *The Academic Forum: The Academic Affairs Publication of New Jersey City University* 10.1 (2001): 27-30.

Chou, Min, and Oliver Zhou. "Academic Libraries and Copyright Protection in a Digital Age." *Proceedings of the International Conference on 'Academic Librarianship in the New Millennium: Roles, Trends, and Global Collaboration.'* Ed. Yong Yang and Haipen Li. Yunnan, China: Yunnan University Press, 2002. 308-318.

Chou, Min, and Oliver Zhou. "Examining the Impact of DMCA and UCITA on Online Reference Service." *Implementing Digital Reference Services: Setting Standards and Making It Real.* Ed. R. David Lankes et al. New York: Neal-Schuman Publishers, Inc., 2003. 47-57.

Determann, Lothar, and Aaron Xavier Fellmeth. "Don't Judge a Sale by Its License: Software Transfers Under the First Sale Doctrine in the United States and the European Community." *University of San Francisco Law Review* 36 (Fall 2001): 1-107.

Diamond v. Diehr, 450 U.S. 63. Sup. Ct. 1981.

Feist Publications, Inc. v. Rural Telephone Service Company, Inc. 499 U.S. 340. Sup. Ct. 1991.

Gasaway, Laura N. "Values Conflict in the Digital Environment: Librarians versus Copyright Holders." *VLA Journal of Law & the Arts* 24 (Fall 2000): 115-161.

Guthrie, Kevin M. "What Do Faculty Think of Electronic Resources." *ALA Annual Conference Participants' Meeting.* 17 June 2001. 16 March 2003. <http://www. jstor.org/about/faculty.survey.ppt>.

Harris, Lesley Ellen. *Licensing Digital Content–A Practical Guide for Librarians.* Chicago, IL: American Library Association, 2002.

Hugenholtz, P. Bernt. "Software as a Commodity: International Licensing of Intellectual Property: Commentary: Copyright, Contract and Code: What Will Remain of the Public Domain?" *Brooklyn Journal of International Law* 26 (2000): 77-90.

Joyce, Craig et al. *Copyright Law,* 5th ed. Newark, NJ: LexisNexis, 2001.

Meyer, Richard W. "Monopoly Power and Electronic Journals." *Library Quarterly* 67.4 (1997): 325-349.

Miller, Rush G. "Shaping Digital Library Content." *Journal of Academic Librarianship* 28.3 (May 2002): 97-103.

"The Need for JSTOR." *JSTOR.* 24 Feb. 2002. 29 Mar. 2003 <http://www.jstor. org/about/need/html>.

ProCD v. Zeidenberg. 86 F.3d 1447. 7th Cir. Ct. 1996.

Schechter, Roger E. "The Unfairness of Click-on Software Licenses." *The Wayne Law Review* 46 (Winter 2000): 1735-1803.

17 U.S.C. §102, §107, §108, §109, §1200, §1201. 2000.

Step-Saver Data Sys. Inc. v. Wyse Technology. 939 F.2d 91. 3rd Cir. Ct. 1991.

Thomas, Sarah. "From Double Fold to Double Bind." *The Journal of Academic Librarianship* 28.3 (2002): 104-108.

Webb, John. "Managing Licensed Networked Electronic Resources in a University Library." *Information Technology and Libraries* 17.4 (1998): 198-206.

Travels into Several Remote Corners of the Information Universe: A Voyage to the Department of the Houyhnhnmists, or, Licensing Issues and the Integrated Collection

Timothy Shipe

SUMMARY. The review and negotiation of license agreements has become a time-consuming but necessary part of the job of providing access to the electronic information resources required by libraries' patrons. The nature of these agreements may pose a number of barriers to the development of fully integrated collections. This article presents a fictitious case-study intended to exemplify a number of the barriers encountered in an academic library during the process of acquiring access to electronic database products. *[Article copies available for a fee from The Haworth Document Delivery Service: 1-800-HAWORTH. E-mail address: <docdelivery@haworthpress.com> Website: <http://www.HaworthPress.com> © 2005 by The Haworth Press, Inc. All rights reserved.]*

KEYWORDS. Electronic information resources, electronic text collections, license agreements

---

Timothy Shipe is Arts and Literature Bibliographer, University of Iowa Libraries, 100 Main Library, Iowa City, IA 52242 (E-mail: timothy-shipe@uiowa.edu).

[Haworth co-indexing entry note]: "Travels into Several Remote Corners of the Information Universe: A Voyage to the Department of the Houyhnhnmists, or, Licensing Issues and the Integrated Collection." Shipe, Timothy. Co-published simultaneously in *The Acquisitions Librarian* (The Haworth Information Press, an imprint of The Haworth Press, Inc.) No. 33/34, 2005, pp. 25-34; and: *Managing Digital Resources in Libraries* (ed: Audrey Fenner) The Haworth Information Press, an imprint of The Haworth Press, Inc., 2005, pp. 25-34. Single or multiple copies of this article are available for a fee from The Haworth Document Delivery Service [1-800-HAWORTH, 9:00 a.m. - 5:00 p.m. (EST). E-mail address: docdelivery@haworthpress.com].

Digital Object Identifier: 10.1300/J101v17n33_03

The story you are about to read is true; the names have been changed to protect the innocent (and to comply with confidentiality provisions).

THE FABLE

The field of Houyhnhnm Studies, a venerable though underfunded discipline within the Humanities, is founded on the study of the fairly limited extant body of transcribed oral texts in the long-extinct Houyhnhnm language. While, like other Humanist scholars, Houyhnhnmists have taken an increasingly interdisciplinary approach to their field, the Houyhnhnm corpus remains the essential primary source for virtually all of their work. Also like their fellow Humanists, Houyhnhnmists (especially the younger generation of scholars) have become increasingly sophisticated in their use of information technology. They are entirely comfortable consulting online catalogs and bibliographic indexes, and participating in scholarly electronic discussion groups. And while they happily leaf through and annotate the pages of the standard critical editions and scholarly translations of the Houyhnhnm texts, the ideal technological tool for them would be a fully searchable, universally accessible yet editorially impeccable electronic version of the Houyhnhnm corpus. Without this tool, from their perspective, the notion of an "integrated collection" is pointless.

So it was with great excitement that scholars received news from the Houyhnhnm Studies Department of the University of Brobdingnag announcing the imminent electronic publication of the complete Houyhnhnm corpus, to be available on floppy disc or CD-ROM as the *Nexus of Electronic Information Gathered for Houyhnhnmists* (NEIGH). As Bibliographer for Classical, Near Eastern and Sentient Equine Languages and Literatures at Lilliput State University, I quickly received several messages from faculty members asking that we purchase this indispensable resource. Although the price was a bit steep for my budget, the need for NEIGH was obvious, and with a little assistance I managed to raise the funds to purchase the database. This was before CD-ROM drives had become standard issue with personal computers, and the Houyhnhnm Studies faculty told me that they preferred that we purchase the floppy disc format, so that they could borrow the discs and make copies for their single departmental computer and for the younger faculty members who owned home computers.

Certainly, this request seemed reasonable in the context of the library models to which the faculty had become accustomed. What is the point of having a primary text if you can't take it to your campus or home office and use it in conjunction with the other scholarly tools at hand–both those borrowed from the University Library and those in your personal library? The concept of an integrated collection requires that information resources be used in conjunction with one another, seamlessly, regardless of format.

Of course, we already knew from experience that electronic databases on disc came with pieces of paper called "licenses." At this stage, we weren't reading them very carefully; someone had heard that since we didn't have to sign the licenses, they weren't binding, and we found it useful to believe that to be true. In those pre-UCITA (Uniform Computer Information Transactions Act) days, we tended to ignore these so-called "contracts of adhesion." ("By breathing within the next ten minutes, you accept the terms and conditions of this agreement; if you do not accept these terms, return this software product to the vendor and hold your breath until you receive acknowledgement and a complete refund.") Even if we had read these licenses carefully, we wouldn't have understood what they were saying. But we were pretty sure that the kind of use the faculty members were proposing was not only a violation of license terms, but also of copyright law–and that wholesale copying of expensive databases by our users was more likely to get us into trouble than the occasional excessive photocopying of printed books and journals over which we had no control. So, we were forced to say "no"–a word which we weren't very comfortable using with our faculty. While the initial reaction of faculty was unpleasant ("fussy librarian" was one of the kinder phrases used), they did ultimately understand our legal and ethical constraints, and we proceeded to purchase the CD-ROM and mount it on a stand-alone machine in our reference area.

NEIGH did receive a fair amount of use, mainly when students had to complete a class assignment designed with NEIGH in mind; at these times, students lined up to use the machine. At other times, the database was little used. The arrangement was hardly conducive to serious research by faculty and dissertation students.

A year later the folks at Brobdingnag started selling a site license permitting various numbers of simultaneous users to have access to the database; around the same time, the technology permitting networking of CD-ROMs within the library building became available. This solved the problem of the queues of students waiting to use NEIGH at busy times, but it was not otherwise any more convenient, and it certainly didn't bring us any closer to offering an "integrated collection" to the Houyhnhnmists on and off campus.

Then NEIGH came up on the World Wide Web. It was now possible to subscribe to (not purchase) this Web version of the database, with no limitation on simultaneous users. The database would be accessible from library, office or home, as long as one was a faculty, staff member, or registered student at the University–and as long as one had the special ID number and password. By this time, scholars had become accustomed to seamless access to electronic resources from home or office. IP-based authentication permitted anyone to use our subscription databases from anywhere on campus, and our secure proxy server allowed authorized users to obtain access from their homes by inputting their university ID numbers. The Houyhnhnmists were itching for this kind of access to the one essential tool of their field. But the nightmare of administering password access to databases was something the library had firmly resisted (with a few exceptions in some of the more lucrative fields supported by departmental librarians). So we again found ourselves in the unpleasant position of saying, if not "no," at least, "please be patient." We suspected that it wouldn't be long before the Houyhnhnmists at Brobdingnag would respond to the demand for IP-based access coming from their increasingly savvy colleagues at other universities. And indeed, it was not long before the announcement came: NEIGH would be offered with IP-based authentication. We placed our order.

THE FABLE TAKES SOME LICENSE

Then came the license. This time, of course, it would have to be signed.

And by now, as it happened, I was not only responsible for selecting materials on various extinct languages and civilizations; I had also been given the responsibility for reviewing and negotiating licenses for electronic resources in all fields, from Armenian Studies to Zoology. I had been to some workshops on license review and negotiation, followed electronic lists on the subject, and felt that I more or less understood what all that legal language was saying and whether the terms were acceptable from the standpoint of the library and its users as well as from the standpoint of the university and its lawyers. I had learned to identify the key areas of likely concern in a vendor's standard license (governing law, indemnification, definition of authorized users, and so forth), and had also learned that vendors are generally willing to make the modifications necessary to enable us to sign the license. Since NEIGH was produced and administered by scholars with an interest in making their product available to their colleagues around the world, and since the license would be an agreement with a state university similar to (albeit vastly larger than) our own, the NEIGH license ought to be an easy matter to resolve.

Wrong.

The license agreement for NEIGH on the Web defined "authorized users" as "students, faculty, and staff of the university," and made no provisions for walk-in users of the library; our library is mandated by state law to be open to the general public, and we do not check the identity of anyone entering our doors. The license permitted authorized users to access NEIGH only through our "secure server," which it defined as a server that authenticates the user's identity; this describes our proxy server for off-campus access, but not the open access to any public computer terminal in the library building. The license stated that the agreement would be governed by the laws of the State of Brobdingnag, and any dispute would be adjudicated in courts located in the city and county of Lorbrulgrud, BG. And there was a clause indemnifying and holding harmless the University of Brobdingnag against any third party legal action connected with our use of NEIGH. The latter two provisions were absolutely unacceptable under Lilliputian law; our university attorneys would never allow the agreement to be signed without changing those provisions, just as the attorneys at Brobdingnag would never permit their librarians to agree to license terms indemnifying another party or granting legal jurisdiction to another state.

So far, this routine was not unusual. I knew the next step: request the necessary changes in the license. I added a provision for walk-in users; I inserted a "notwithstanding" clause to avoid the issue of on-campus authentication; I changed "State of Brobdingnag" to "State of Lilliput" and "Lorbrulgrud, BG" to "Mildendo, LP" (figuring that if that were not acceptable, we could compromise by leaving the agreement silent on the issue of governing law); and I deleted the fatal indemnification clause. These solutions had almost always been acceptable to our vendors.

But not to the University of Brobdingnag. Heaven knows, it was not the fault of the Houyhnhnmists who were responsible for NEIGH. They were at the mercy of their university's attorneys, and those attorneys were subject to various policies of the university. Among those policies was one that stated that all contracts must include a clause indemnifying the University of Brobdingnag against third-party lawsuits–a provision that made it virtually impossible to sell the Web version of NEIGH to any state university. Furthermore, frankly, the university attorneys had much bigger fish to fry; they did not have time to waste negotiating a contract that was only of interest to scholars in an obscure field of the Humanities that didn't bring the University any money worth mentioning.

Meanwhile, it was becoming a challenge to explain to our own faculty what the delay was about. Copyright was a concept they understood and accepted, but that the arcane legal language of contracts–governing law, indemnification, and the like–could have anything to do with their seamless access to ancient Houyhnhnm texts was almost too much to bear.

There was a happy ending. Eventually, so many university libraries had to refrain from the purchase of this essential resource, to the chagrin of so many Houyhnhnmist colleagues, that the faculty members at Brobdingnag were able to persuade their legal office to make a few modifications in the contract language that made it possible for most libraries (including our own) to sign the agreement and obtain Web access to the database. Now our scholars are able to integrate this online corpus into their research routine, in tandem with the bibliographical and critical tools of their trade, whether in print or online. They can do this from machines in the library, in their departmental offices, or in the comfort of their homes, surrounded by their dusty print editions of specific texts, their drawers full of notebooks and index cards. NEIGH is now comfortably becoming part of the scholarly environment in which they work. Of course, since they have had this access for only a few months, they have yet to quote from NEIGH in their own publications. When they do, they may be surprised to realize that the form of their citations will be determined not by the standard bibliographic guide they have used for their entire scholarly careers, but by a legally binding contract that tells them exactly how their citation must be formatted.

THE LICENSE IN THE REAL WORLD

What is the truth behind this fable? Obviously, "NEIGH" does not represent any one database, but rather a conflation of experiences many of us have had in licensing a number of different databases in the humanities. And the narrative is fairly representative of the general evolution of our adaptation of different phases of information technology into the context of our library, and of the parallel evolution of our handling of the license agreements which govern our use of that technology. The licensing issues that have been mentioned comprise no more than a sampling of the various concerns that may typically arise as we negotiate an agreement.

Once we have resigned ourselves to paying the price of a product (perhaps after negotiating some kind of reduction), most licensing issues can be resolved to the mutual satisfaction of library and licensor. There have been very few electronic resources (assuming that we could afford them) that we have had to forgo because of irresolvable license issues. However, it is unfortunately the case that the most fundamental resources in a few fields have been the ones that have presented the greatest challenges to the librarians negotiating the licenses. Ironically, these have generally not been commercial products, but databases owned and distributed by academic institutions. Perhaps this has happened because the small scale of the scholars' operation forces them to adopt license terms drawn up for them by institutional attorneys who have no stake in the marketability of the product.

BARRIERS TO INTEGRATED ACCESS

How does licensing affect our efforts to implement the integrated collection?

Clearly, a major barrier to the integrated collection is created when we are unable to provide access to an essential resource because of irreconcilable licensing disagreements. However, apart from issues of pricing, in the six years I have been reviewing licenses for my institution, this has only happened twice. The real barrier that most licenses present to creating a truly integrated collection is their very status as contracts that are binding on the entire institution and on each of its students and faculty members.

In essence, licenses tend to force scholars to follow different sets of rules and guidelines than they would follow for print resources. A scholar may, for example, have come to a fairly sophisticated understanding of copyright law and the rights and responsibilities that law establishes in connection with the fair use of published material. But a license agreement may "trump" copyright law and its fair use provisions, giving the user of a database fewer rights and more responsibilities than he or she would have in the absence of the license. Furthermore, a license agreement may specify the exact format of any citation to the database in a published article or monograph, and this format may well differ from the Chicago or MLA citation style with which the scholar is most likely familiar. And unless these terms appear on screen when the scholar uses the database, the library is placed in the almost impossible position of having to somehow inform the user of these special license provisions whenever they differ from normal scholarly practice.

We try to avoid this problem by changing any license language that imposes requirements that differ from normal, responsible, ethical scholarly behavior. For the avoidance of doubt, we often request the addition of a clause to the effect that nothing in the agreement will be interpreted to limit the rights granted under the fair use provisions of United States Copyright Law. But if the licensor is unwilling to accept these modifications, we are faced with the difficult situation of scholars having to follow different sets of rules for apparently similar resources. This hardly makes for a truly integrated collection.

An additional barrier to the integrated collection occurs when a license grants no permanent rights to use the data. When we first started thinking about issues of ownership versus access, many of us conceived this as a dichotomy between physical ownership of a document and remote access to an information resource located on a remote computer. If we came to accept the "access" model for certain kinds of information resources (such as bibliographic databases), it was because we felt it was important to provide our users with access to information whenever they needed it, regardless of where the physical resource was located. But as the kinds of available electronic resources expanded beyond continually updated bibliographic databases to things like full-text corpora, many of which were essentially closed bodies of information such as the fictitious NEIGH, we began to become more concerned with the notion of archival rights. "Ownership" came to signify not physical custody of a resource, but permanent rights to use that resource wherever it is located. When some producers of full-text databases in the Humanities began moving to a subscription model whereby we would lose all access if we stopped paying the annual fee, this distinction became clear to us. And if canceling a journal subscription meant losing access to back issues, we wondered how long it would be before we would be asked to send back our bound back runs of any journals for which we cancelled a print subscription. It would be hard for a scholar to view print and electronic collections as an integrated whole if large portions of the electronic collection might disappear during a fiscal crisis. Attempting to secure permanent rights to use the data for which we pay has become a major priority in our license negotiations. However, there are significant electronic resources for which we are unable to secure such rights.

This creates a sense of uncertainty about the enduring nature of some of our resources, an uncertainty that seriously undercuts the goal of the integrated collection.

In summary, appropriately crafted license agreements are essential in order for us to provide the electronic side of the integrated collection. But at the same time, difficulties with license agreements may create serious barriers to the implementation of the integrated collection. These barriers appear to fall into three broad categories. First, an inability to conclude an agreement because of irreconcilable disagreements (such as a licensor's unwillingness to change terms that are illegal under the licensing library's state laws) may force the library to exclude a key information resource from its collection. Second, an inability to modify license terms that impose unusual restrictions or requirements on use may force the library's clientele to use different resources in different ways; a researcher may no longer be able to rely on his or her knowledge of customary, ethical scholarly practices with respect to such issues as copyright, fair use, and even citation format. Third, an inability to negotiate license terms that grant archival access may create a sense of impermanence in the library's integrated collections, a sense that a resource on which a scholar relies may be here today and gone tomorrow.

Like Lemuel Gulliver, librarians have been exploring uncharted territory during the past several decades, visiting countries whose laws and customs pose a challenge to our frame of reference. But if the present imperfect version of the integrated collection presents a landscape as disappointing to us as that which England presented to Gulliver upon his return from the country of the Houyhnhnms, I think that we have shown that we are not inclined, like Gulliver, to retreat into splendid isolation from a flawed information society, but will rather continue to make every effort to make the licenses we negotiate work for, rather than against, the emerging ideal of the integrated collection.

SELECTED RESOURCES

This essay is not intended to be a comprehensive survey of issues connected with license review and negotiation, nor is it intended to constitute legal advice. Readers seeking an overview of these issues are referred to two excellent Web sites on library licensing issues. The LIBLICENSE site at Yale University <http://www.library.yale.edu/~llicense/index.shtml> provides the most comprehensive introduction to the topic, including license terminology and typical license terms, model licenses, links to other Web resources, and an extensive bibliography. LIBLICENSE also hosts an electronic discussion list on library licensing issues. The Association of Research Libraries also hosts a Licensing Issues site at <http://www.arl.org/scomm/licensing/index.html>. These pages include information on the licensing workshops organized by ARL and held at various locations around the country. These workshops are highly recommended for any librarian with responsibilities in the area of license review and negotiation.

REFERENCE

Swift, Jonathan. *Travels into Several Remote Nations of the World, in Four Parts, by Lemuel Gulliver*. London: Benj. Motte, 1726. Eighteenth-Century Fiction Full-Text Database. Chadwyck-Healey. 19 March 2003. <http://lion.chadwyck.com>.

OPINIONS, RESEARCH, AND ANALYSIS

Harvesting for Disseminating: Open Archives and the Role of Academic Libraries

Eugenio Pelizzari

SUMMARY. The scholarly communication system is in a critical stage, due to a number of factors. The Open Access movement is perhaps the most interesting response that the scientific community has tried to give to this problem. The paper examines strengths and weaknesses of the Open Access strategy in general and, more specifically, of the Open Archives Initiative (OAI), discussing experiences, criticisms and barriers.

All authors that have faced the problems of implementing an OAI compliant e-print server agree that technical and practical problems are not the most difficult to overcome and that the real problem is the change

Eugenio Pelizzari is Director, Interfaculty Central Library of Economics and Law, University of Brescia, Italy (E-mail: pelizzar@eco.unibs.it). He is attending the Ma/MSc International Information Studies promoted by the University of Northumbria (UK) and the University of Parma (Italy).

[Haworth co-indexing entry note]: "Harvesting for Disseminating: Open Archives and the Role of Academic Libraries." Pelizzari, Eugenio. Co-published simultaneously in *The Acquisitions Librarian* (The Haworth Information Press, an imprint of The Haworth Press, Inc.) No. 33/34, 2005, pp. 35-51; and: *Managing Digital Resources in Libraries* (ed: Audrey Fenner) The Haworth Information Press, an imprint of The Haworth Press, Inc., 2005, pp. 35-51. Single or multiple copies of this article are available for a fee from The Haworth Document Delivery Service [1-800-HAWORTH, 9:00 a.m. - 5:00 p.m. (EST). E-mail address: docdelivery@haworthpress.com].

http://www.haworthpress.com/web/AL
Digital Object Identifier: 10.1300/J101v17n33_04

35

in cultural attitude required. In this scenario, the university library is possibly the standard bearer for the advent and implementation of e-prints archives and Open Archives services. To ensure the successful implementation of this service the Library has a number of distinct roles to play. *[Article copies available for a fee from The Haworth Document Delivery Service: 1-800-HAWORTH. E-mail address: <docdelivery@haworthpress.com> Website: <http://www.HaworthPress.com> © 2005 by The Haworth Press, Inc. All rights reserved.]*

KEYWORDS. Self-archiving, Open Access archives, Open Archives Initiative

INTRODUCTION

The "anomalous picture" described in an important paper (Harnad, "For Whom") is a fine example of the critical point in which scholarly communication lies.

The ever increasing journal prices, perceptions of inadequacies in the journal system, along with a consistent reduction in library resources and the advent of new technologies, thus creating new opportunities, have all contributed to a ferment of innovative ideas and projects for enhancing or replacing the present scholarly communication system.

The crisis has a paradoxical aspect: scientists and researchers who produce this specialist literature, mainly with the aid of external public investments, grant their articles to the editors without gaining any revenues. Later on, when trying to use them, they face serious problems of access. The first response to this crisis has come from the LIS community. After an initial reactive phase, characterized by subscription cancellations and increasingly intensive adoption of the "just in time" strategy, it has resulted in a number of initiatives with the goal of modifying the scholarly communication process, "freeing" scientific literature from the "chains" of lucrative commercial publishers.

The Open Access initiatives are perhaps the most interesting response that the scientific community has tried to give to this problem.

OPENING ACCESS TO SCHOLARLY COMMUNICATION

What does the word "open" mean in the context of digital libraries? At least two different interpretations are possible and both of them work towards the enhancement of scholarly communication, though from different points of view.

From one point of view, "open" means "free accessibility through the Web to the contents of refereed articles, now, for all, forever," its most enthusiastic supporter being Stevan Harnad.

In his criticism (together with other "activists" of the so-called Electronic Publishing Reform Movement, e.g., Paul Ginsparg and Andrew Odlyzko) of the traditional scholarly communication system, Harnad has been resetting his initial intuition of an electronic-only model of scholarly publications (Duranceau, 111). Since his first proposal, new topics have been examined, presented and discussed internationally (such as costs, archiving, preservation, quality control and the role of commercial publishers) and new solutions offered. Perhaps the most complete view of his model is outlined in the paper in which he presents his idea and contrasts supporters of opposing views (Harnad, "E-Knowledge").

Through Harnad's vision the model (based on a non-peer-reviewed pre-prints world) applies now only to the refereed journal literature, not to other types of scholarly communication such as books, best-sellers, etc. The first essential distinction he poses is between "non-give-away" literature and "give-away" literature. In the latter, authors do not seek fees for their work; they only seek research "impact" on the scientific community (also for career reasons). Until now, dissemination has been guaranteed by publishers that recover costs restricting access to those who can pay (academic and research libraries). Harnad claims that in an electronic-only environment, the costs can be drastically reduced and recovered by authors (or by other actors) rather than subscribers, so that users can access scientific literature free of charge on the Internet.

Harnad recommends that online public self-archiving of refereed journals can and should be introduced without delay and he sees it as "optimal and inevitable" in all fields within a very short time.

However, Harnad himself recognizes that his "original 'subversive proposal' of freeing the refereed literature through auto self-archiving fell largely on deaf ears because self-archiving in an anonymous FTP archive or a Web home page would be unsearchable, unnavigable, irretrievable, and hence unusable. Nor has centralized archiving, even when made available to other disciplines, been catching on fast enough either" (Harnad, "Self-Archiving").

At this point, the second approach to the term "open" as it is intended–and declared–by the Open Archives Initiative (OAI; http://

www.openarchives.org/) is raised: "Our intention is 'open' from the architectural perspective–defining and promoting machine interfaces that facilitate the availability of content from a variety of providers. Openness does not mean 'free' or 'unlimited' access to the information repositories that conform to the OAI-PMH" (OAI–Protocol for Metadada Harvesting; http://www.openarchives.org/documents/FAQ.html).

The term "interoperability" is not a new concept. In June 2000, Paul Miller discussed that almost all-pervasive term, interoperability, and distinguished six possible types of interoperability: technical, semantic, political/human, inter-community, legal and international. He discussed what it really means to be interoperable, concluding that: "A truly interoperable organization is able to maximise the value and reuse potential of information under its control. It is also able to exchange this information effectively with other equally interoperable bodies, allowing new knowledge to be generated from the identification of relationship between previously unrelated sets of data. Changing internal systems and practice to make them interoperable is a far from simple task. The benefits for the organization and those making use of information it publishes are potentially incalculable" (Miller, "Interoperability").

The Open Archives Initiative has now provided the metadata tagging standards that enable the content of distributed archives to be interoperable.

In this sense, the Self-Archiving Initiative (http://www.eprints.org) is devoted to opening access to the refereed research literature online, providing free software for institutions to create OAI-compliant archives, interoperable with all other open archives through the OAI–Protocol for Metadata Harvesting (http://www.openarchives.org/OAI/openarchivesprotocol.html).

The concept behind this initiative is: free accessibility.

Attention has been focused on the importance of open archiving for scientists in poorly-resourced countries (Chan and Kirsop, "Open Archiving").

THE OPEN ARCHIVES INITIATIVE

In its original form, the UPS (Universal Preprint Service), a type of self-archiving which focused on unrefereed pre-prints, was quickly dropped and the Open Archives Initiative has since vastly outgrown those limited original objectives (Van de Sompel and Lagoze, "The Santa Fe").

The OAI has hence become (despite its original core aim) a much broader initiative than the Self-Archiving Initiative. OAI is now providing shared interoperability standards for the entire online digital literature world, whether self-archived or not, free or for a fee, be it a journal, a book or other, full text or not, centralised or distributed. The concept behind this initiative is: interoperability.

Although OAI is still in its early phases, "it is gaining significant momentum and it is predicted to become a key piece of the future digital library landscape" (Breeding, "Emergence").

The roots of OAI lie in the e-print community; it arose from a meeting held in Santa Fe in 1999 (Van de Sompel and Lagoze, "The Santa Fe") to discuss mechanisms to encourage the development of e-print archives and solutions. ArXiv (http://arxiv.org/), the physics e-print archive, run by Paul Ginsparg, had already changed the publishing paradigm in its field (Ginsparg, "Creating"). The group attending this meeting were investigating the possibility of extending these changes to other domains. The outcome of this meeting was the development of the technical and organizational agreement known as the Santa Fe Convention and the adoption of an interoperability solution known as "metadata harvesting" (Lagoze and Van de Sompel, "The Open Archives").

During the numerous workshops held following the Santa Fe meeting, it emerged that many other groups had very similar problems to those faced by the e-print community: "the metadata that each community wanted to make available had unique features, but the underlying mechanism of making metadata available for harvest was widely needed" (Shearer, "Open Archives").

With the above criteria in mind an international steering committee was set up to develop the initiative. Its goal was to support the harvesting of all kinds of metadata and to explore other technical problems related to metadata harvesting and other potentially valuable application.

In September 2000, OAI extended its interoperability framework beyond e-prints to facilitate the dissemination of the contents. This framework was named "OAI Protocol for Metadata Harvesting."

THE OAI PROTOCOL FOR METADATA HARVESTING
(OAI-PMH)

The Open Archives Initiative Protocol for Metadata Harvesting (OAI-PMH) was released in January 2001, substituting an initial protocol that resulted from the Santa Fe meeting (Warner, "Exposing"). The protocol "is simply an interface that a networked server (not necessarily an e-print server) can employ to make metadata describing objects housed at that server available to external applications that wish to collect this metadata" (Lynch, "Metadata Harvesting"). In July 2001, the protocol was updated to incorporate XML-related standards.

Version 1.x of OAI-PMH was experimental, and the results over the following sixteen months seemed to indicate that its underlying technical scope was properly defined. On June 1st 2002, version 2.0 was officially released.

Herbert Van de Sompel and Carl Lagoze state that during the period from the first to the second release the protocol has emerged as a practical foundation for digital libraries' interoperability. The reasons for OAI-PMH's vast approval by the scientific community can be seen in the light of a number of factors: it is low barrier, exploiting widely deployed Web technologies; it builds on metadata practice, leveraging the development of a lingua franca metadata vocabulary in the Dublin Core Metadata initiative (http://dublincore.org); it accommodates different communities and domain-specific extensions (Van de Sompel and Lagoze, "Notes," 144). The initiative is seen by other authors as the right framework to build Open Digital Libraries (Suleman and Fox, "Framework").

From a technical point of view the protocol is http-based and uses the "Get or Post" mechanism. "Repositories" are defined as networked accessible systems that contain metadata that can be harvested. The metadata is returned encoded in XML (Needleman, 156).

Two types of participants are defined: data providers and service providers. Following the OAI definitions: "A data provider maintains one or more repositories (Web servers) that support the OAI-PMH as a means of exposing metadata," while "a service provider issues OAI-PMH requests to data providers and uses the metadata as a basis for building value-added services" (http://www.openarchives.org/documents/FAQ.html). In fact, "While resource discovery is often mentioned as the exemplar service, other service possibilities include longevity and risk management, personalization and current awareness" (Van de Sompel and Lagoze, "Notes," 144).

OPEN ARCHIVES INITIATIVE: A WORK IN PROGRESS

The–relative–simplicity of the OAI-PMH Protocol has attracted a large number of "repositories" (or "archives"). The list of registered repositories as of 03/10/2003 stands at sixty-five, including e-print servers, digital library collections, electronic theses and dissertations archives and so on, with contents offered in a variety of media (http://OAIsrv.nsdl.cornell.edu/Register/BrowseSites.pl), while at the same date there are twelve registered service providers that provide services based on metadata that is harvested using the OAI Metadata Harvesting Protocol (http://www.openarchives.org/service/listproviders.html). Registration is voluntary for both OAI compliant data and service providers and it is also possible that not all repositories or service providers have registered with the OAI.

Peter Suber wrote: "Institutional eprint archiving is currently undergoing an unprecedented surge of acceptance and support. Eprint archiving has three components:

1. the software for building the archives, E-prints for large institutional or disciplinary archives and Kepler for smaller individual 'archivelets' (Maly, Zubair and Liu, 'Kepler');
2. the Open Archives Initiative metadata harvesting protocol, the standard for making the archives interoperable, and
3. the decision by universities and laboratories to launch archives and fill them with the research output of their faculty" (Suber, "Momentum").

On the Free On-Line Scholarship Newsletter (FOS; http://www.earlham.edu/~peters/fos/), referring to the previous six months, he lists the major developments on these three fronts stating that: "If you've been following the progress of the FOS movement for any number of years, you'll agree that no other single idea or technology in the movement has enjoyed this density of endorsement and adoption in a six month period" (Suber, "Momentum").

In theory, this should be true but, on the other hand, according to the number of data and service providers registered, and from the insufficient spread of non-OAI compliant e-print archives we can argue that this new paradigm is not so completely shared and accepted by the scientific community. Practical implementation of open archives can perhaps help us to understand the barriers that hinder the full development of their potentialities.

OPEN ARCHIVES:
EXPERIENCES, CRITICISMS, AND BARRIERS

While there has been a lot of publicity about the Open Archives Initiative as an idea, there has been much less on the actual implementation of OAI archives and the problems it faces. Criticisms have arisen concerning both the technical and the more general cultural aspects.

Technical Concerns

Kathleen Shearer observes that "the key debate about the value of the protocol is regarding the granularity of its metadata" (Shearer, "Open Archives"). The Open Citation Project (OpCit; http://opcit.eprints.org/) promoters, for example, believe that "it does not provide a rich enough infrastructure on which to build services, such as a reference linking" and have proposed "extending the current OAI framework to include access to full text content of archived data, rather than simply the location of a document." The objection is that "expanding minimum metadata standard will discourage participation by data providers, thus limiting the scope and ultimately the power of the OAI Protocol for Metadata Harvesting." Furthermore, according to Lynch, any implementation of the OAI-PMH at an institutional level should be done by consulting with other institutions, along with a careful consideration as to what metadata will be exposed and its particular level of granularity, regarding the future use of this metadata (Lynch, "Metadata Harvesting").

Powell, discussing the openness of the Protocol, states that the use of the existing mechanism can be adopted (for example, by publishers) to restrict access to the contents (Powell, "An OAI Approach"). However, this could possibly be considered one of the protocol's strengths, whose degree of accessibility can be freely decided by those implementing it.

More General Concerns

Stephen Pinfield, in two important articles, examines how print archives are used (Pinfield, "How Do Physicists") and the implications in setting up an institutional OAI compliant e-print archive (Pinfield, Gardner and MacColl, "Setting Up").

The following are some of his concerns:

- The format of papers: careful consideration must be given to what formats will be accepted from authors, what formats they will allow on the e-print server and whether they can, if necessary, convert from one format to another.
- Metadata format and quality: this is crucial to the OAI Service Providers who are harvesting it and creating search facilities. The creators of the ARC service (an experimental service provider), for example, report a number of problems associated with metadata diversity (Liu, Maly and Zubair, "Arc").
- The need to standardize metadata so as to enable more consistent retrieval of results from cross-collection searches has been confirmed in a paper describing a recent work carried out by the University of Illinois Library, recipient of one of seven OAI-related grants from the Andrew W. Mellon Foundation (Cole et al., "Now That").
- One more possible weakness of the OAI protocol related to metadata is the fact that the OAI metadata is not picked up by conventional search engines. This possibility is being discussed in the "OAI-general" discussion list (http://oaisrv.nsdl.cornell.edu/pipermail/oai-general/) and in the September 1998 American Scientist Forum (http://amsci-forum.amsci.org/archives/september98-forum.html). New software tools such as DP9, which can translate OAI compliant metadata into search engine-friendly data, may be important (http://arc.cs.odu.edu:8080/dp9/index.jsp).
- Subject scheme seems to be a very important issue. Nixon states that while a local scheme may be very useful for local use there is the need to use an established subject scheme which would provide some degree of consistency for future cross-searching (Nixon, "Evolution").
- Authentication and long-term preservation of documents: this aspect is of particular importance to the "open archives" community. These problems have not been looked into by the Open Archives Initiative. Data providers remain responsible for the preservation and accuracy of their records. As Mayfield states, perhaps "the most difficult issue that universities face in building their own repositories is in upending age-old processes such as peer review" (Mayfield, "College Archives"), although research on possibilities for connecting peer review with archive servers and interoperability with publishing workflow processes are being carried out (Bentum et al., "Reclaiming").

- The self-submission process: the self-submission process (that eprint.org software allows) may create some problems. Pinfield argues that some potential contributors may lack the know-how or the patience to submit their documents themselves. In the initial stages of the implementation of institutional archives, it may be best if the archive administrator inserts papers on behalf of users (Pinfield, Gardner and MacColl, 2002). Not all users, in fact, will wish to self-archive their material for a variety of reasons–from time constraints to technical ability–but it is seen as vital to provide this as an option (Nixon, 2002).
- "Look and feel": Pinfield states that institutional design polices have an impact on the "look and feel" of the archives, suggesting that they have the same consistent look and feel of other existing resources such as catalogues. Cole and his colleagues suggest identifying likely users of the system as distinctly separate groups adopting consequently different end-user search interface design strategies (Cole et al., "Now That").
- Another question raised is how a directory of OAI compliant repositories will be maintained. The method currently in use provides a list of self-registered archives that can work with few repositories but will not be sufficient as the number of repositories increases (Shearer, "Open Archives").
- From a practical implementation point of view, William Nixon states that, in his experience with the institutional e-prints archive at the University of Glasgow, the technical expertise which computing services provided was essential in getting the archive up and running (Nixon, "Evolution").
- Difference in fields: a shared opinion is that there are basic differences among the scientific fields that influence the acceptance of the open archives philosophy and their use (Relman, 1828). Some authors state that the variety of practices seem to be related to specific fields, based on particular work products, and that "communicative heterogeneity" will persist (Kling and McKim, "Not Just"). In mathematics, for example, the use of Tex language facilitated the diffusion of free accessible documents, while this has not occurred in other fields. As De Robbio affirms, behaviour can also be different inside the same particular field, as with mathematicians, where communications are sometime shared by e-mails and not deposited in archives. Moreover, in the IT field, researchers are used to putting their works on personal sites and Web pages rather than in archives: this fragmentation hinders the establish-

ment of a common strategy towards open archives (De Robbio, "Open Archives").

On the other hand it is said that institutional repository policies, practices, and expectations must also accommodate the differences in publishing practices between academic disciplines (Crow, "Case").

Cultural Barriers

All authors that have faced the problems of implementing an OAI-compliant e-print server agree that technical and practical problems are not the most difficult to overcome and that the real problem is the change in cultural attitude required by professors and researchers.

William Nixon confirms this idea: "the challenge, ultimately will not be the technical implementation of an e-prints service but rather the cultural change necessary for it to become embedded and commonplace in the activities of the institution." Also for this reason, he claims that change should be assisted by national programmes and international declarations such as that of the Budapest Open Access Initiative (BOAI; http://www.soros.org/openaccess/).

Suzie Allard stresses the need to develop structures like OAI, to understand the human and social dimensions as well as the technology. The psychological aspect, in terms of finding procedures that are comfortable for individuals with different approaches to the information environment, has to be carefully considered as well, stating that "humanities scholars approach research in an entirely different fashion than researchers in the hard sciences. Each group would be very uncomfortable with the other's technique, yet each group can generally conduct a satisfactory search" (Allard, "Erasing").

Jeffrey R. Young, investigating barriers to the implementation of open archives, found that the biggest obstacle may be inertia. He reports the opinion of Mrs. MacKenzie Smith, Associate Director of Technology for MIT's libraries, on the super archive which has been developed at the Massachusetts Institute of Technology, called Dspace (http://www.dspace.org/): "Professors are busy, and they may not use the repository if they perceive it as more work, even if they like it in principle. Setting up the framework for an archive was the easy part, however. Getting professors to contribute is proving more difficult." "It's a slow process," confirms Eric F. Van de Velde, Director of Library Information Technology at Caltech. "We talk to people all the time" to try to get them to include material, he adds. "This is not foremost on the mind of any faculty member, and changing the work flow kind of takes time" (Young, "Superarchives").

The same concept is expressed by Raym Crow, SPARC Senior Consultant: "The greatest obstacle to any change in the fundamental structure of scholarly communication lies in the inertia of the traditional publishing paradigm (Crow, "Case").

These assumptions have been confirmed by two surveys.

The Information World Review reports about a survey conducted with their scientific panelists (not an academic environment) where they were asked if they saw self-archiving by authors as a means of solving some of the problems in scientific journal publishing.

Overall, sixty percent of respondents saw self-archiving as an idea worthy of consideration. However, within this group, less than a third were wholehearted supporters, while the rest felt it was too soon to be able to predict how successful self-archiving might be. Forty percent expressed real reservations.

The most common objections raised were: that authors preferred to be published in recognised channels for the sake of their careers, that they could not be relied upon to be consistent in their approach, or find the time for self-archiving ("Jury is Still Out").

However, most panelists' doubts were cultural, the two most often cited being career progression and the problem of overturning established practices ("Panelists Have Doubts").

More interesting, though, is a survey on attitudes and perceptions regarding e-publishing carried out among academic staff of the three universities participating in the ARNO Project (http://cf.uba.uva.nl/en/projects/arno/).

The results showed that perceptions regarding institutional open archives as a parallel publication channel vary a lot among the different fields, suggesting that programs and projects for encouraging their use should be tailored to accommodate these differences.

Concerns about copyright were confirmed, along with the importance of a "quality label for academic output" (Bentum et al., "Reclaiming").

DISCUSSION

All the opinions set out in the literature seem to confirm that "setting an archive up is one thing, getting users to participate in its ongoing development is quite another" (Pinfield, Gardner and MacColl, "Setting Up").

The problems seem to be related more to cultural aspects rather than to technological or developmental issues.

The participation of users is required both through the contribution to contents, and to the use of e-print archives; the problem may also be that users will not use the archive until there is a sufficient content but they won't contribute content until they use it.

An important step is seen in talking to academics and scholars more generally about scholarly communication issues. An OAI-compliant e-print archive is not to be seen as an isolated development but as a response to a number of structural problems in the academic publishing field.

It is quite probable that scholars are not as interested as librarians are in the "serials crisis" problem. Rising costs can easily be seen as a "librarians' problem." Possibly, it is more effective to emphasize the arguments more related to researcher activities: among them lowering impact barriers, ease of access, rapid dissemination, OAI functionality and valued added services.

Previous experience suggests a better chance of success when positioning the repository as a complement to, rather than as a replacement for, traditional publishing.

There are a number of major concerns that academics seem to raise on a regular basis:

- Intellectual property rights (and particularly copyright)
- Quality control (and particularly peer review)
- Workload (their own)
- Undermining the "tried and tested" publishing status quo (on which academic reputations and promotions lie)

In this sense, organizing special promotional events for university staff might be very important.

As a paradox: Elsevier does allow its authors to publish their papers in institutional repositories or in other non-commercial archives, provided that the authors first ask permission. Arie Jongejan, chief executive officer of Elsevier Science and Technology, a division of Reed Elsevier, says that fewer than five percent of authors ask.

Harnad explains that the reason is that disciplines fields are not the right agent for change: "The right entity for all of this is the university" (Young, "Superarchives").

THE ROLE OF LIBRARIES

The university library is possibly the standard bearer for the advent and implementation of e-prints archives and Open Archives services. To ensure the successful implementation of this service the library has a number of distinct roles beyond its technical know-how and maintenance. These have been identified as the following (Nixon, "Evolution"):

- Encouraging authors of the University to deposit material in the e-prints archives;
- Providing advice to authors about copyright and journal embargo policies for material which they would like to deposit in the archive, and liaising where required directly with the journal;
- Converting material to a suitable format such as HTML or PDF to import into the archive and ensuring that HTML which is submitted is properly formatted and cross-browser compatible;
- Depositing material directly on behalf of members of the University who do not, or cannot self-archive their scientific publications.

In this new scenario the role of the library changes, as affirmed by the SPARC Position Paper: "Establishing an institutional repository program indicates that a Library seeks to move beyond a custodial role to contribute actively to the evolution of scholarly communication" (Crow, "Case").

Peter Suber states: "The Internet has given scholars and librarians an unprecedented opportunity to save money and advance their interests at the same time. We should simply seize it. What are waiting for?" (Suber, "Removing").

More sensationally, Barbara Quint declares: "This is the best chance librarians will ever have to break the chains that have bound them and their budgets. . . . Who will step up and help to create a better process of scholarly communication? Who will do the hard work and take the risks? . . . If academic librarians do not step up to pay that price and right now, they could find themselves blocked out of that future and perhaps any future at all . . . ACT. Now or never" (Quint, "Now or Never!").

REFERENCES

Allard, Suzie. "Erasing the Barrier Between Minds: Freeing Information, Integrating Knowledge." *American Communications Journal* 4.2 (2001). 10 March 2003 <http://www.acjournal.org/holdings/vol4/iss2/articles/allard.htm>.

Bentum, Maarten van, Renze Brandsma, Thomas Place and Hans Roes. "Reclaiming Academic Output Through University Archive Server." *The New Review of Information Networking* 7 (2001). 10 March 2003 <http://drcwww.kub.nl/~roes/articles/arno_art.htm>.

Breeding, Marshall. "The Emergence of the Open Archives Initiative." *Information Today* 19.4 (2002): 46-47. Business Source Premier, EBSCO, Biblioteca Centrale Interfacoltà di Economia e Giurisprudenza dell'Università degli Studi di Brescia, Italia. 10 March 2003 <http://search.epnet.com/>.

Chan, Leslie and Barbara Kirsop. "Open Archiving Opportunities for Developing Countries: Towards Equitable Distribution of Global Knowledge." *Ariadne* 30 (2001). 10 March 2003 <http://www.ariadne.ac.uk/issue30/oai-chan/intro.html>.

Cole, Timothy W., Joanne Kaczmarek, Paul F. Marty, Christopher J. Prom, Beth Sandore and Sarah Shreeves. "Now that We've Found the 'Hidden Web,' What Can We Do with It." *Museums and Web 2002.* 10 March 2003 <http://www.archimuse.com/mw2002/papers/cole/cole.html>.

Crow, Raym. "The Case for Institutional Repositories: A SPARC Position Paper." *SPARC* (2002). 10 March 2003 <http://www.arl.org/sparc>.

De Robbio, Antonella. "Open Archives. Per Una Comunicazione Scientifica 'Free Online.'" *Bibliotime* 5.2 (2002). 10 March 2003 <http://www.spbo.unibo.it/bibliotime/num-v-2/derobbio.htm>.

Duranceau, Ellen Finnie. "Resetting Our Intuition Pumps for the Online-Only Era: A Conversation with Stevan Harnad." *Serials Review* 25.1 (1999): 109-15.

Ginsparg, Paul. "Creating a Global Knowledge Network." *Second Joint ICSU Press–UNESCO Expert Conference on Electronic Publishing Science–Session 'Responses From the Scientific Community'* [2001]. 10 March 2003 <http://arxiv.org/blurb/pg01unesco.html>.

Harnad, Stevan. "E-Knowledge: Freeing the Refereed Journal Corpus Online." *Computer Law and Security Report* 16.12 (2000): 78-87. 10 March 2003 <http://www.cogsci.soton.ac.uk/~harnad/Papers/Harnad/harnad00.scinejm.htm>.

———. "For Whom the Gate Tolls? How and Why to Free Refereed Research Literature Online Through Author/Institution Self-archiving, Now." (2001). 10 March 2003 <http://www.cogsci.soton.ac.uk/~harnad/Tp/resolution.htm>.

———. "The Self-Archiving Initiative." *Nature* 410 (2001): 1024-25. 10 March 2003 <http://www.nature.com/nature/debates/e-access/Articles/harnad.html>.

"Jury is Still Out on Open Archives." *Information World Review* 179 (2002): 1. Business Source Premier, EBSCO, Biblioteca Centrale Interfacoltà di Economia e Giurisprudenza dell'Università degli Studi di Brescia, Italia. 10 March 2003 <http://search.epnet.com/>.

Kling, Rob and Geoffrey McKim. "Not Just a Matter of Time: Field Differences and the Shaping of Electronic Media in Supporting Scientific Communication." *Journal of the American Society for Information Science* 51.14 (2000): 1306-1320. 10 March 2003 <http://www.webuse.umd.edu>.

Lagoze, Carl and Herbert Van de Sompel. "The Open Archives Initiative: Building a Low-Barrier Interoperability Framework." (2001). 09 April 2003 <http://www.openarchives.org/documents/oai.pdf>.

Liu, Xiaoming, Kurt Maly and Mohammad Zubair. "Arc–An OAI Service Provider for Digital Library Federation." *D-Lib Magazine* 7.4 (2001). 10 March 2003 <http://www.dlib.org/dlib/april01/liu/04liu.html>.

Lynch, Clifford A. "Metadata Harvesting and the Open Archives Initiative." *ARL Monthly Report* 217 (2001). 10 March 2003 <http://www.arl.org/newsltr/217/mhp.html>.

Maly, Kurt, Mohammad Zubair and Xiaoming Liu. "Kepler–An OAI Data/Service Provider for the Individual." *D-Lib Magazine* 7.4 (2001). 10 March 2003 <http://www.dlib.org/dlib/april01/maly/04maly.html>.

Mayfield, Kendra. "College Archives 'Dig' Deeper." *Wirenews* (2002). 10 March 2003 <http://www.wired.com/news/print/0,1294,54229,00.html>.

Miller, Paul. "Interoperability. What Is It and Why Should I Want It." *Ariadne* 24 (2000). 10 March 2003 <http://www.ariadne.ac.uk/issue24/interoperability/intro.html>.

Needleman, Mark. "The Open Archives Initiative." *Serials Review* 28.2 (2002): 156-58.

Nixon, William. "The Evolution of an Institutional E-Print Archive at the University of Glasgow." *Ariadne* 32 (2002). 10 March 2003 <http://ariadne.ac.uk/issue32/eprint-archives/intro.html>.

"Panelists Have Doubts About Science Publishing Experiment." *Information World Review* 179 (2002): 3. Business Source Premier, EBSCO, Biblioteca Centrale Interfacoltà di Economia e Giurisprudenza dell'Università degli Studi di Brescia, Italia. 10 March 2003 <http://search.epnet.com/>.

Pinfield, Stephen. "How Do Physicists Use an E-Print Archive?" *D-Lib Magazine* 7.12 (2001). 10 March 2003 <http://www.dlib.org/dlib/december01/pinfield/12pinfield.html>.

Pinfield, Stephen, Mike Gardner and John MacColl. "Setting Up an Institutional E-Print Archive." *Ariadne* 31 (2002). 10 March 2003 <http://www.ariadne.ac.uk/issue31/eprint-archives/intro.html>.

Powell, Andy. "An OAI Approach to Sharing Subject Gateway Content." (2001). In *Proceedings Tenth International World Wide Web Conference*, Hong Kong. 10 March 2003 <http://www10.org/cdrom/posters/1097.pdf.>.

Quint, Barbara. "Now or Never!" *Searcher* 10.1 (2002). 10 March 2003 <http://www.infotoday.com/searcher/jan02/voice.htm>.

Relman, Arnold S. "The NIH 'E-Biomed' Proposal. A Potential Threat to the Evaluation and Orderly Dissemination of New Clinical Studies." *The New England Journal of Medicine* 340.23 (1999): 1828-29.

Shearer, Kathleen. "The Open Archives Initiative. Developing an Interoperability Framework for Scholarly Publishing." *CARL/ABRC Backgrounder Series* 5 (2002). 10 March 2003 <http://www.carl-abrc.ca/projects/scholarly/open_archives.PDF>.

Suber, Peter. "Momentum for E-print Archiving." *FOS Newsletter.* 08/08/2002. 20 February 2003 <http://www.topica.com/lists/suber-fos/read/message.html?mid=1607391538&sort=d&start=39>.

_____"Removing the Barriers to Research: An Introduction to Open Access for Librarians." *College & Research Libraries News* 64 (February 2003): 92-94, 113. The print edition is abridged. An online unabridged edition is available at <http://www.earlham.edu/~peters/writing/acrl.htm>. Last visited 10 March 2003.

Suleman, Hussein and Edward A. Fox. "A Framework for Building Open Digital Libraries." *D-Lib Magazine* 7.12 (2001). 10 March 2003 <http://www.dlib.org/dlib/december01/suleman/12suleman.html>.

Van de Sompel, Herbert and Carl Lagoze. "Notes from the Interoperability Front: A Progress Report on the Open Archives Initiative." *Proceedings of the 6th European Conference, ECDL 2002.* Rome, Italy, September 16-18, 2002. Berlin: Springer-Verlag, 2002. 144-57. 10 March 2003 <http://link.springer.de/link/service/series/0558/papers/2458/24580144.pdf>.

_____"The Open Archives Initiative: Building a Low-Barrier Interoperability Framework." *Proceedings of the First ACM/IEEE-CS Joint Conference on Digital Libraries.* New York: ACM Press, 2001. 54-62. 10 March 2003 <http://www.openarchives.org/documents/oai.pdf>.

_____"The Santa Fe Convention of the Open Archives." *D-Lib Magazine* 6.2 (2000). 10 March 2003 <http://www.dlib.org/dlib/february00/vandesompel-oai/02vandesompel-oai.html>.

Warner, Simeon. "Exposing and Harvesting Metadata Using the OAI Metadada Harvesting Protocol." *HEP Libraries Webzine* 4 (2001). 20 February 2003 <http://library.cern.ch/HEPLW/4/papers/3>.

Young, Jeffrey R. "'Superarchives' Could Hold All Scholarly Output." *The Chronicle of Higher Education* 48.43 (2002). 10 March 2003 <http://chronicle.com/free/v48/i43/43a02901.htm>.

The Electronic Librarian: Inching Towards the Revolution

Emerita M. Cuesta

SUMMARY. Electronic resources are transforming the way librarians work. New technological skills have been added to the librarian's tool kit. Some libraries have undertaken large-scale organizational reconfigurations to meet the challenges of the digital environment. Yet libraries still rely on traditional functions such as acquisitions, cataloging, and reference. This paper examines job advertisements published online between January 2001 and March 2003 to determine the degree of overlap between traditional and electronic duties in the modern library organization, and draws some conclusions about the state of the digital library. *[Article copies available for a fee from The Haworth Document Delivery Service: 1-800-HAWORTH. E-mail address: <docdelivery@haworthpress.com> Website: <http://www.HaworthPress.com> © 2005 by The Haworth Press, Inc. All rights reserved.]*

KEYWORDS. Professional development, electronic resources, digital libraries, library organization, technology

Emerita M. Cuesta is Assistant Director for Technical Services and Acquisitions Librarian, University of Miami Law Library, Coral Gables, FL 33149 (E-mail: ecuesta@law.miami.edu).

[Haworth co-indexing entry note]: "The Electronic Librarian: Inching Towards the Revolution." Cuesta, Emerita M. Co-published simultaneously in *The Acquisitions Librarian* (The Haworth Information Press, an imprint of The Haworth Press, Inc.) No. 33/34, 2005, pp. 53-62; and: *Managing Digital Resources in Libraries* (ed: Audrey Fenner) The Haworth Information Press, an imprint of The Haworth Press, Inc., 2005, pp. 53-62. Single or multiple copies of this article are available for a fee from The Haworth Document Delivery Service [1-800-HAWORTH, 9:00 a.m. - 5:00 p.m. (EST). E-mail address: docdelivery@haworthpress.com].

53

INTRODUCTION

AACR2, 2002 revision, defines an electronic resource as "material (data and/or program(s)), encoded for manipulation by a computerized device" (Weitz, "Cataloging Electronic Resources"). Hidden behind this innocuous description is a radical transformation in the concept of information. With it comes a no less radical transformation in the definition of librarianship. In a paper published in 1996, Peter Young described the job of the librarian in the revolutionary digital environment:

> Although librarians have traditionally engaged in the organization and arrangement of information collections, digital collections and services call for librarians to function as knowledge navigators, or, as some have suggested, as cyberspace organizers. The nature of digital information resources also requires digital librarians to be resource integrators and to offer users customized consultation and interpretation services. The new digital information environment requires that librarians add value to the use of information. Librarians working in digital information structures are creators of information through the assembly, organization, and generation of new knowledge. (Young, 124)

The change in the role of librarians in the academic environment was explored in a study by Anne Woodsworth and Theresa Maylone that compared jobs in libraries and computing centers. Sixty-three distinct job descriptions were analyzed to determine the similarities in a number of factors, including skills and responsibilities. They found that there were several areas of total or partial overlap, including user services, resource collection, support services, and system analysis and design. The authors concluded that a single job family was emerging that included both library and computing positions (Woodsworth and Maylone, 7).

However, despite the accelerating pace of change created by information technology, the library must continue to manage traditional collections and provide traditional services. Books and journals must be ordered, cataloged, and checked-in; the reference desk must be manned. Too often it seems as if electronic resources simply add another layer of complexity to the old job, as each new technology requires a new set of skills that must be acquired. The need to cope has given rise to a new library specialty: the Electronic Resources Librarian.

This paper will look at jobs using "electronic" as part of the job title to determine how libraries are integrating duties relating to electronic resources into their workflow. Specifically, it explores whether the kind of organizational change predicted by Young, Woodsworth, and Maylone, among many others, has taken place.

LITERATURE REVIEW

Several content analysis studies have been carried out exploring the technological component of job descriptions. Of these, three recent ones have examined the development of "electronic" positions in academic libraries. In 2000, Beile and Adams analyzed 900 job announcements published in major library publications in 1996 using the techniques developed by Reser and Schuneman in 1992. They found that in order to conduct a proper analysis, they had to expand Reser and Schuneman's divisions of public services and technical services to include a third division, electronic services, that would accommodate systems, automation, and electronic services positions. They found that, although all positions analyzed required some degree of computer expertise, electronic resources and services positions were found to have more detailed technical requirements than those in the other two divisions (Beile and Adams, 3).

In 2001, Lynch and Smith analyzed 200 job advertisements appearing in *College and Research Library News* between 1973 and 1998. In addition to reference and administrative positions, they analyzed a third group that incorporated several traditionally separate duties such as cataloging, collection development, and reference, into a single job description. Lynch and Smith found that the combination positions "demanded and expected professionals to have computer skills as part of their general background and preparation" (Lynch and Smith, 11).

The third paper analyzed positions that explicitly used the terms "electronic" and "digital" as part of the job title. Karen Croneis and Pat Henderson reviewed 223 advertisements published in *College and Research Library News* between January 1990 and December 2000 using four criteria: position title, functional area, institution, and year of publication. A subset of 50 advertisements all dating from 2000 was then analyzed in depth.

Although geared to determining the similarities and differences between "electronic" and "digital" positions, the study provides a fascinating view of a decade of librarianship:

A public service position (Electronic Instruction Librarian at the University of Virginia) was the first advertisement to appear in this study. The emphasis on public services continued for a number of years. Specifically, the number of positions with primary responsibility in public services increased from one in 1990, one in 1991, five in 1992, eight in 1993, 10 in 1994 and 21 in 1995. For the first three years studies (1990-1992), all identified positions were in public services. Initial announcements for non-public services areas appeared in 1993 (technical services), 1995 (systems), and 1997 (digital projects). (Croneis and Henderson, 236)

When focusing on the 2000 positions, Croneis and Henderson found that, of the jobs using "electronic" in the title, 50% included reference, 41.6% included instruction and training, 35.3% included collection development, 23.5% included cataloging, and 20.6% included acquisitions. They do not indicate which of these duties related specifically to electronic resources or also involved traditional services, however, in their conclusion they state that "many jobs in this study still include responsibilities for what might be viewed as traditional activities such as reference and instruction, albeit in technologically sophisticated surroundings" (Croneis and Henderson, 236).

THE ELECTRONIC LIBRARIAN TODAY

Although the papers cited above address job responsibilities rather than reporting lines, it is clear that today's electronic librarians are spread throughout the library organization. This small study set out to determine whether these positions reflected major organizational redesign or were incorporated into a traditional library structure.

Job advertisements published in several major online venues, such as ALA job ads, the C&RL Job Ads, the EDUCAUSE Job Posting Service, and IFLA's LibJobs were used. Duplicates were eliminated as were position descriptions for public and special libraries. A sample of 50 jobs was acquired, all representing academic libraries and academic law libraries in the United States and Canada. They are analyzed for four factors: title, reporting lines, functional area of primary job responsibility, and traditional components.

Primary Responsibility

Results show that since 2001, "electronic resources" job advertisements posted on professional Web sites have been skewed towards Technical Services functions. Of the 50 jobs analyzed, 28 were for positions whose primary responsibility fell in the areas of cataloging, acquisitions, serials, and systems. Whether this was due to the online environment or whether it is a true reversal in direction from that noted by Croneis and Henderson was not pursued, as it is not within the purview of this paper; however, it merits further study.

Reporting Lines

Slightly over half of the advertisements (29) listed a reporting line. Of these, 27 fell comfortably within some variation of the traditional library structure. Librarians reported to the Director/Chief Librarian (3), Head of Cataloging (7), Head of Reference/Research/Information Access (4), Head/Coordinator of Acquisitions (6), Serials/Periodicals Librarian (3), Head of Technical Services/Bibliographic Control (3), and Assistant Director for Collection Services (1). Only two positions reflected a true structural change: one reported to the Faculty Director for Electronic Resources Development and Information Delivery, and one reported to the Director of Metadata Services.

Traditional Duties

In determining traditional duties, the job descriptions were analyzed for specific references to services such as reference desk rotation, general or subject bibliographic instruction, subject bibliography, and faculty liaison duties. It was found that all but five of the job advertisements had some component of traditional services not directly related to electronic resources, as seen in Table 1.

This data suggests that technology-driven organizational change is not occurring at the predicted rate nor taking the expected route.

Electronic versus Traditional Duties

Results show that the majority of library jobs are still solidly centered on traditional duties such as reference, collection development, acquisitions, and cataloging. A cursory look at the job requirement section of the advertisements reveals, however, that all librarians are expected to

TABLE 1

	Technical Services Positions	Public Services Positions
Reference	6	12
Acquisitions	6	0
Collection Development	5	4
Serials Cataloging	8	0
Non-Print Formats Cataloging	9	0
Bibliographic Instruction	1	9
Faculty/Departmental Liaison	3	2
Subject Bibliographer	2	0

have expertise in computer-based library tools, as well as database and Web searching skills.

Job versus Institutional Restructuring

While many of the jobs advertised crossed public/technical services boundaries, the reporting line breakdown indicates that libraries are still more likely to be organized along traditional lines. Restructuring seems to be happening much more rapidly at the individual position or the intradepartmental level than at the institutional level. This result would support Lynch and Smith's conclusion that "organizational changes have begun to appear at the more entry-level jobs where departmental and unit team environments are mentioned. This was expected because the reference and the combination jobs were beginning to show change in content and changing jobs generally are expected to be organized into different structures. However, the administrative job ads did not reflect change in organizational structure" (Lynch and Smith, 418).

Public versus Technical Services Positions

As the table above shows, the technical services positions posted are more likely to cross traditional boundaries than the public services positions. Serials and acquisitions librarians and catalogers were more likely to participate in reference, liaison and instructional programs, while no public services librarians had duties involving traditional technical services work. This seems to indicate that restructuring is occurring at two different rates within the organization.

These results must be considered tentative until in-depth studies are carried out. However, they confirm that today's electronic librarian positions are overwhelmingly hybrid entities, still managing print collections and providing traditional services while simultaneously attempting to develop and maintain digital resources.

TRAFFIC BUMPS ON THE ROAD TO REVOLUTION

In *The Final Encyclopedia*, science-fiction author Gordon Dickson envisions a massive computer that contains the accumulated knowledge of all mankind. During the heady early days of technological explosion, the most enthusiastic proponents of the information revolution seemed to suggest that libraries would be transformed into nodes of a world-wide cyber-encyclopedia that would provide access to all knowledge at the click of a mouse. In turn, this vision was embraced by university administrators who saw technology as a way to maintain a high level of information delivery in the face of flat or declining budgets.

This vision has not come to pass as expected. Although it is impossible to deny that technology has brought radical change into the library, it has done so not as a replacement for traditional work, but as a facilitator of and addendum to it. We can readily identify several reasons for this:

Cost

The promised budgetary savings associated with technology have not materialized. Libraries have been forced to make electronic resources access decisions that involve considerable shifting of funds away from one format to the other, or from one resource to the other. On the publishing front, the cost of conversion has proved a handicap to wholesale retrospective digitization. This means that for the foreseeable future academic libraries will still need to maintain print collections in order to meet the needs of researchers and students.

Copyright

This issue still remains a long way from settled. Publishers and librarians have not been able to come to an agreement as to what represents fair use in the electronic environment. Libraries currently subsidize electronic access through purchase of full-text databases and one-time payments for reprints. As long as this conflict is not resolved, however, unlimited online access to scholarly information remains out of reach.

Technological Change

Ironically, the vertiginous rate of evolution of new storage and access technologies has inevitably created uncertainty. Few libraries have the time, staff, and funds to spend on each new product. All we can do is make informed guesses about the staying power of each, and invest accordingly.

Discipline Differences

Some academic disciplines are much more likely to adopt information technology than others. They use the library and its resources in markedly different ways. Libraries must be responsive to both.

Human Resistance

Although many in academia have embraced the technology revolution, just as many are doubtful, if not downright hostile. Some of these people can be found among the library's most influential clientele. Libraries often have to negotiate the middle ground between the technophobes and technophiles in their institutions.

CONCLUSIONS

Academic libraries are in a transitional period. Although the advocates of the digital library have proven a bit too optimistic, it is true that technology has dramatically transformed basic definitions such as "collection" and "access." Within the constraints described above, which vary from institution to institution, libraries are integrating electronic resources and services into their collections and developing new selection and management models to accommodate them. Most have embarked on some kind of restructuring, whether at the position, departmental, or institutional level. Nevertheless, there is still a need for traditional functional services such as acquisitions, cataloging, reference, and circulation, and these duties are not likely to vanish in the foreseeable future.

This fluid environment is clearly reflected in the introduction of the "electronic resources librarian." With duties ranging from selecting and licensing electronic databases to answering questions at the reference desk, these librarians must be proficient at multitasking in several environments. They must be technologically expert and knowledgeable about one or more academic disciplines. They must manage departments, administer budgets, teach undergraduates, and negotiate with vendors. They are the ultimate example of librarians as polymaths.

However, it remains to be seen whether the electronic librarian is the interim step to a completely new paradigm of librarianship or simply will remain yet another format-based specialty with "other duties as assigned." The assortment of duties in each job description and the number of different reporting lines point to the fact that while electronic resources are being rapidly assimilated into the library, electronic librarianship is still at best an experiment.

The emergence of the electronic resources librarian as a specialty also obscures the fact that we are all electronic librarians these days. Technology is part and parcel of our daily lives. Some technology skills are so common that proficiency has become an unspoken assumption. One of the most consistent job requirements is some variation on the statement "knowledge of and experience with a wide array of electronic tools and resources." It implies a continuous learning cycle that impacts every librarian working everywhere, from a single-person operation to the largest university research library. While this was true to some extent in the print environment, the speed at which we must learn has taken a quantum jump. That is where the real revolution lies.

REFERENCES

Beile, Penny M., and Megan M. Adams. "Other Duties as Assigned: Emerging Trends in the Academic Library Job Market." *College and Research Libraries* 61:4 (Jl 2000). Wilsonweb Omnifile, University of Miami Law Library, March 31, 2003 <http://vnweb.hwwilsonweb.com>.

Consortium for Educational Technology for University Systems. *The Academic Library in the Information Age: Changing Roles.* California: The Trustees of the California State University, 1997.

Croneis, Karen S., and Pat Henderson. "Electronic and Digital Library Positions: A Content Analysis of Announcements from 1990 through 2000." *The Journal of Academic Librarianship* 28:4 (Ju 2002): 232-237.

Lynch, Beverly P., and Kimberley Robles Smith. "The Changing Nature of Work in Academic Libraries." *College and Research Libraries* 62:5 (S 2001): 407-420.

Simmons-Wellburn, Janice. *Changing Roles of Library Professionals.* SPEC Kits #256. Washington, DC: Association of Research Libraries, May 2000.

Weitz, Jay. *Cataloging Electronic Resources: OCLC-MARC Coding Guidelines.* April 9, 2003 <http://www.oclc.org/connexion/documentation/type.htm>.

Woodsworth, Anne, and Theresa Maylone. *Reinvesting in the Information Job Family: Context, Changes, New Jobs, and Models for Evaluation and Compensation.* CAUSE Professional Paper Series, #11. Colorado: CAUSE, 1993. March 27, 2003 <http://www.educause.edu/asp/doclib/abstract.asp?ID=pub3011>.

Young, Peter R. "Librarianship: A Changing Profession." Books, Bricks, and Bytes. *Daedalus: Journal of the American Academy of Arts and Sciences*, (F 1996): 103-125.

The Method Behind the Madness: Acquiring Online Journals and a Solution to Provide Access

Donna Skekel

SUMMARY. Libraries are seeking the best possible solution for integrating online journals into their collections. While exploring the different methods and technology available, many libraries still strive to fulfill the original "library mission" proposed by Charles Cutter in his *Rules for a Dictionary Catalog*. Providing comprehensive access to scholarly journals and individual journal articles becomes increasingly difficult with the advent of journal subscription vendors, general and subject-specific databases, and even journal management software and services aimed at helping libraries manage journal changes and the representation of their holdings to patrons in their public catalogs. Although libraries have found it necessary and desirable to acquire a wide range of journal databases and services, many anticipate that advancements in technology and cooperative efforts among the many institutions and interests involved will eventually allow easier and widespread cross-data-

Donna Skekel is Serials/Cataloging Librarian, Musselman Library, Gettysburg College, 300 North Washington Street (Campus Box 420), Gettysburg, PA 17325 (E-mail: dskekel@gettysburg.edu).

[Haworth co-indexing entry note]: "The Method Behind the Madness: Acquiring Online Journals and a Solution to Provide Access." Skekel, Donna. Co-published simultaneously in *The Acquisitions Librarian* (The Haworth Information Press, an imprint of The Haworth Press, Inc.) No. 33/34, 2005, pp. 63-71; and: *Managing Digital Resources in Libraries* (ed: Audrey Fenner) The Haworth Information Press, an imprint of The Haworth Press, Inc., 2005, pp. 63-71. Single or multiple copies of this article are available for a fee from The Haworth Document Delivery Service [1-800-HAWORTH, 9:00 a.m. - 5:00 p.m. (EST). E-mail address: docdelivery@haworthpress.com].

63

base searching for resource discovery and the type of patron access to journal literature that is desired. *[Article copies available for a fee from The Haworth Document Delivery Service: 1-800-HAWORTH. E-mail address: <docdelivery@haworthpress.com> Website: <http://www.HaworthPress.com> © 2005 by The Haworth Press, Inc. All rights reserved.]*

KEYWORDS. Electronic journals, online journals, journal management software, cataloging, journal access, library patrons, databases, aggregators, journal subscriptions, journal vendors, e-journal collections, scholarly research, subject access

A PATRON SHOULD BE ABLE TO FIND AN ITEM IF . . .

When Dr. Ezra Abbott and Charles Cutter were industriously working on their innovative card catalog at Harvard in the 1860s, they probably were not thinking about providing access to individual articles in newspapers, magazines, and journals, yet these are the very resources many researchers and students want to consult. What is the latest research, or what has been written recently about a specific topic? What are the experts in the field saying about a particular subject? What has a certain author written on a subject? As librarians we naturally want to follow Cutter's *Rules*, and technology is helping us achieve this, even as collections and the numbers of resources available to libraries grow. A study at one academic institution showed that 84 percent of faculty and students who responded preferred e-journals to print journals (Montgomery and King, "Comparing Library"). However, the current state of implementing journal management software and juggling different electronic databases and vendors sometimes makes us wish we could go back in time to be with Ezra and Charles, meticulously writing on 3 × 5 catalog cards.

Are libraries able to fulfill the original, basic "library mission" proposed by Charles Cutter in his *Rules for a Dictionary Catalog*? Journal management software products and services are attempting to help libraries manage their serials by gathering, producing, and maintaining listings of the electronic journals that are available at each institution, so library holdings are accurately reflected in the online public catalog. Though just at the beginning of implementing Serials Solutions at our small liberal arts college library, this consolidation of all our online journals at one Web page location is already an improvement over many journal titles remaining "hidden" in databases. It provides patrons with an alphabetical journal title list with links to the databases that contain each online journal. Another alphabetical listing of all our print journal holdings has recently been added. With a separate search box provided on our library Web site for the Serials Solutions journals, patrons can search for journals. If our patrons know the journal title or ISSN they are searching for, they can find it through Serials Solutions. However, subject searching is not available for this compilation of all our full-text e-journals, and this will be the next major focus for our library–to provide better subject access to these online journals. Journal management software may not be a definitive "solution," but it beats the cost and labor-intensive staff time involved for individual subscriptions to thousands of journals and numerous publishers, and it provides a central location for displaying all the journal titles that are in the library's collection. Also, part of the Serials Solutions service (yearly fee involved) includes incorporating any journal changes, additions, or deletions and updating our journal holdings information accordingly . . . things are getting better. Though Serials Solutions does not do *everything* we might want it to, it does much more than we could do alone, and we have so far been able to provide access to full-text electronic (and print) journals by title or ISSN in one location on our library's Web site.

It seems that most libraries are well on their way to providing e-journal collections for their patrons–an important service, especially for academic libraries–often by using a journal management tool. However, now the priority switches to gaining bibliographic control of electronic journals. Catalogers look at databases and think of how to approach these new and useful electronic resources. To MARC, or not to MARC, the question keeps coming. Ideally, we want patrons to perform literature searches using the library catalog, perhaps a keyword or subject search that would retrieve every relevant scholarly journal article the library has obtained access to for its collection. So far, this dream has not come true. There are quite a few makers of electronic "search applications" (e.g., Paratext's WebFeat, Auto-Graphics' AGent, Google's Search Appliances) that offer a customized, consolidated search engine to interface with institutional, online, and Web-based databases and electronic resources. There are also many and various open source software options available (e.g., see "open source systems for libraries" at <oss4lib.org>, or "koha open source library system" at <koha.org>). Being able to employ one of these applications for improved searching capability across different databases is very appealing, as libraries want "linkability": we want seamless links to each information target and then a neat display of the most relevant results. But the reality of implementing such a system is much less appealing; what we may suspect and find from a purchased (or free) software solution and/or service is that it is not as "interoperable" and "seamless" as we had hoped. We want to purchase a solution, push the start button, and have it work immediately, problem-free. Some libraries are "home-growing" their own subject access systems and achieving various levels of subject access for patrons, as recently described in an article by Gerry McKiernan in *Library Hi Tech News*. Our cataloging staff has always added its own college-assigned "subject series" links to MARC records in the catalog, so that relevant resources may be grouped together and displayed for each academic department. This serves as a research aid to students, who can click on the appropriate link to see a list of resources for a particular subject, as well as "nearby titles." The displayed MARC catalog records also contain subject links that will lead patrons to a list of "nearby subjects." However, unless there is already a MARC record in the catalog for a journal in the library's holdings, it is not possible to implement these methods for all the electronic journals contained in the databases provided by vendors, subscription agents, and/or Serials Solutions.

Providing research aid by cross-database subject access to individual journals through keyword searching may be where libraries are headed. Libraries did not provide subject access to print journals in the past, especially not to each journal's content and individual articles. But now that journals are available electronically, and we *could* in the future provide indexed keyword searching (as Google does), should we? If this type of searching were provided, would it merely overwhelm patrons with the large number of retrieved choices that bewilder current users of Internet search engines who often never look past the first page of results? (Wolfram et al., "Vox Populi," 1073). Many library patrons naturally want to "google" a topic in the library's catalog, which is their equivalent of a subject search. Our most recent library catalog usage statistics show that the majority of searches (for the previous academic fall semester) were keyword searches. Even the number of subject searches nearly tripled the number of searches by journal title. However, providing a successful keyword searching function would require top-notch precision and recall, as the public continues to have a low tolerance of wading through pages and pages of retrieved search results (Wolfram et al., "Vox Populi," 1073).

THE "MAD" SCIENTISTS

While we are concerned with providing the most beneficial access to e-journal articles for library patrons, there are many authors of e-journal articles and researchers, such as Peter Suber, who are concerned with "removing the barriers to research." Suber and others have been discussing the task of working toward open access initiatives and institutional repositories for peer-reviewed literature.

> The difference between free and fee-based access is the difference between a seamless, completely interlinked learned literature at the fingertips of every scholar and scientist in the world and a jerry-rigged agglomeration of toll-ridden proprietary packages–the online counterparts of exactly what we have now in the trade world of scholarly paper journals, funded through Subscriptions, Site-Licenses and Pay-Per-View . . . (Harnad, "For Whom")

Though the World Wide Web and the Internet have made scholarly communication more timely (particularly in interpersonal communications), publisher-inflicted embargoes on journals can result in frustration when access to recently published scholarly literature is restricted in a publication for which an individual or institution does not have a current subscription. Publishers, whether of print and/or electronic information, are mostly *for*-profit entities. However, many publishers are now adopting liberal self-archiving policies for their contributing authors, which result in less restricted access for authors and researchers. The Eprints movement is having an effect. Project RoMEO (Rights MEtadata for Open archiving) has compiled and posted a list of existing journal publisher copyright transfer agreements (Oppenheim, "Project RoMEO"), indicating which publishers support open archiving and to what degree. But even self-posting and archiving research literature for others to access can be costly. Some institutions may have the electronic means and infrastructure in place to aid in these initiatives, but working for scholarly access in this way also requires more faculty time and a permanent staff to steward the growing collection of research literature. It requires the proper equipment (and updating) and staff to archive and provide access to individual works.

For now, we are left with our "jerry-rigged agglomeration of toll-ridden proprietary packages"–and that is exactly what it feels like to librarians. Many libraries have already given up some selection or collection development control of e-journals (due to budgetary considerations) for the trade-off of having aggregators and database vendors communicate with publishers and maintain the changes in titles and publication dates (relieving many library staff hours for other functions and operations). Perhaps a library does not obtain the exact biological research journal title requested on its list of preferred purchases for one fiscal year–but the vendor provided three extra free titles on the same subject! The library community seems to face continually escalating costs for electronic resources–both the cost of the resources themselves and the staff to acquire and provide access to these resources. Some sacrifices are made to offset cost increases. Journal vendors and subscription services are almost a necessity with the large number of journals that need to be processed and made available to patrons. The other option (individual, direct subscriptions for *all* journals) would result in very high costs in staff time.

Libraries are caught in a bit of a quagmire. While possibly anticipating that technology will provide the ideal solution for all our electronic resource access problems, what do we do in the meantime? The title of a recent *Serials Librarian* article by Martin and Hoffman poses an important question: Do we catalog or not? We find ourselves hurrying to revise rules and learn new guidelines for cataloging serials and electronic resources, when basic assumptions of cataloging are being questioned. Roy Tennant tells us in a *Library Journal* article that MARC must die. Should we revise MARC, instead of revising MARC rules? Is technology changing too fast, or not fast enough? How much money do you spend on something while you're waiting for the next wave of technology to happen and for something better to come along?

LIBRARIES AND TECHNOLOGY: A PERFECT MATCH

Some librarians are slightly ashamed that they refer patrons to amazon.com for book summaries and customer opinions and the "customers who bought this book also bought" functions of Amazon's Web site. *Encyclopaedia Britannica*, which almost missed getting on the information highway a while back, can now display on one Web page a searcher's term defined in several ways, descriptions, links to magazine and journal articles, "The Web's Best Sites" on the subject, and videos and media sources about the search term. It all displays nicely, in columns like a newspaper, with accompanying graphics (try searching on "clouds" at britannica.com). The searcher can see what information is available in all formats. Can we do this with MARC? Should we want to? We are, after all, in the "business" of preserving and archiving for the long-term; we are not merchants, selling information or our current inventory. However, we are also no longer limited to just machine-readable cataloging; the "machine" has come a long way, and MARC should grow and change with it. Remember the computer programming languages, FORTRAN and COBOL? Sound ancient? They still have their uses today, but computers and computer programmers have moved on to new and better computing languages. MARC could be renovated while still maintaining its bibliographic integrity for storing and retrieving creative works.

Libraries might even consider implementing some of the features found in retail and information markets, and truly embrace integrating resources in various formats into their collections and catalogs, as well as acquiring some value-added services. It would be satisfying to search on a subject and see a display of everything the library (not the Internet) has on the subject–including videos, journals, etc., as seen on the search pages of britannica.com. Another desirable feature, "topic tracker," is offered by encyclopedia.com. Researchers wishing to stay up-to-date on a topic click the "track this topic" button to the right of an article and receive weekly e-mails about recently published articles on their topic. What a great way to serve a patron feeling overwhelmed with the amount of information to wade through, or, to serve a well-informed patron who is familiar with everything written on a topic except what is currently being published. Library patrons might also be pleased with some well-known features found on amazon.com, such as "e-mail a friend about this item" (already implemented by some libraries) and "search for similar books by subject" (subject assistance that is not "buried" at the bottom of a MARC record display as in many library catalogs). There are many ways that technology can enhance a patron's resource discovery, especially for electronic journals, as detailed in an article by McKiernan in *The Serials Librarian*.

There is no doubt that technology has served us and our patrons well, and will continue to expand our ability to provide access to all types and formats of information in the future. Remote access used to be the bookmobile. Computer technology, even with all its frustrating details to work out, is *good*. Access is improved. Convenience is better than ever. Technology will likely play a major part in allowing complete (author, title, and subject) access to all library materials, so that some day we will know and show exactly "what the library has on a given subject" (Cutter, 12). We are almost there. Perhaps, soon, the library MARC will get a makeover. It may be true that it is catalog *design* we have neglected since leaving the card catalog (Elrod, "Re: MARC"). Yet function and design go hand in hand.

No matter how large or small a library is, librarians do strive for quality and want to provide the best information resources to support their particular library communities. Acquiring and providing access to library materials in integrated formats requires a constant eye on new technology and the employment of a wide range of methods for storage and retrieval, such as aggregated e-journal collections, individual periodical subscriptions, electronic databases (some organized by subject, others more general), e-book collections, shared resources through a consortium, inter-library loan services, remote access through the Internet, electronic document delivery, in-person and online research help, in-person and online reference help, in-house and online reference resources, information literacy classroom instruction, in-person and online library tutorials, Web-based subject portals and resource links, in-house and digital access to special collections or archived materials, microfiche, microfilm, in-house use of laptops, print materials and/or other physical items on reserve, electronic reserves, cassette tapes, VHS video tapes, CD-ROMs, DVDs, and oh, yes–books on shelves.

REFERENCES

Cutter, Charles Ammi. *Rules for a Dictionary Catalog.* 4th ed. Rewritten. Washington: Government Printing Office, 1904.

Elrod, J. McRee. "Re: MARC Requiem, Part 2." Online posting. 18 November 2002. AUTOCAT Online Cataloging Forum. 9 Mar. 2003 <http://listserv.buffalo.edu/cgi-bin/wa?S1=autocat&X=->.

Harnad, Stevan. "For Whom the Gate Tolls? Freeing the On-Line-Only Refereed Journal Literature." Online posting. 25 Aug. 1998. American Scientist E-Print Forum. 30 Jan. 2003 <http://www.ecs.soton.ac.uk/~harnad/Hypermail/Amsci/0000.html>.

Martin, Charity K., and Paul S. Hoffman. "Do We Catalog or Not? How Research Libraries Provide Bibliographic Access to Electronic Journals in Aggregated Databases." *The Serials Librarian* 43.1 (2002): 61-77.

Montgomery, Carol Hansen, and Donald W. King. "Comparing Library and User Related Costs of Print and Electronic Journal Collections." *D-Lib Magazine* 8.10 (2002). 20 Mar. 2003 <http://www.dlib.org/dlib/october02/montgomery/10montgomery.html>.

Suber, Peter. "Removing the Barriers to Research: An Introduction to Open Access for Librarians." Earlham College (2003). 28 Jan. 2003 <http://www.earlham.edu/~peters/writing/acrl.htm>.

Tennant, Roy. "MARC Must Die." *Library Journal* (2002). 11 Feb. 2003 <http://libraryjournal.reviewsnews.com/index.asp?layout=articlePrint&articleID=CA250046>.
Wolfram, Dietmar, Amanda Spink, Bernard J. Jansen, and Tefko Saracevic. "Vox Populi: The Public Searching of the Web." *Journal of the American Society for Information Science and Technology* 52.12 (2001): 1073-1074.

SELECTED RESOURCES

Banerjee, Kyle. "How Does XML Help Libraries?" *Computers in Libraries* 22.8 (2002) 3 Sept. 2002 <http://www.infotoday.com/cilmag/sep02/Banerjee.htm>.
Block, Marylaine. "Beat Out by Amazon." *Ex Libris* 85 (2001). 22 Mar. 2003 <http://marylaine.com/exlibris/xlib85.html>.
McKiernan, Gerry. "E Is for Everything: The Extra-Ordinary, Evolutionary [E-] Journal." *The Serials Librarian* 41.3/4 (2002): 293-321.
McKiernan, Gerry. "Library Database Advisors–Emerging Innovative Augmented Digital Library Services." *Library Hi Tech News* 19.4 (2002) 24 Feb. 2003 <http://fidelio.emeraldinsight.com/vl=12609686/cl=48/nw=1/rpsv/journals/lhtn/eprofile1.htm>.
Oppenheim, Charles. "Copyright Policies." *Project RoMEO (Rights MEtadata for Open archiving)*. 2002-2003. Dept. of Information Science, Loughborough U. 28 Mar. 2003 <http://www.lboro.ac.uk/departments/ls/disresearch/romeo/>.
Tennant, Roy. "Digital Libraries–Cross-Database Search: One-Stop Shopping." *Library Journal* (2001). 7 Oct. 2002 <http://libraryjournal.reviewsnews.com/index.asp?layout=articlePrint&articleID=CA170458>.
Tennant, Roy. "Library Catalogs: The Wrong Solution." *Library Journal* (2003) 4 Mar. 2003 <http://libraryjournal.reviewsnews.com/index.asp?layout=articlePrint&articleID=CA273959>.

SYSTEMS AND SOFTWARE

Choices in Cataloging Electronic Journals

Cecilia A. Leathem

SUMMARY. Libraries and catalogers face choices in the treatment of the growing collections of electronic journals. Policies issued by CONSER and the Library of Congress allow libraries to edit existing print records to accommodate information pertaining to the electronic versions (single record option) or to create new records for them. The discussion describes each option and considers the advantages and disadvantages of both choices. *[Article copies available for a fee from The Haworth Document Delivery Service: 1-800-HAWORTH. E-mail address: <docdelivery@haworthpress.com> Website: <http://www.HaworthPress.com> © 2005 by The Haworth Press, Inc. All rights reserved.]*

KEYWORDS. Serials cataloging, electronic journals, single record option, online catalogs

Cecilia A. Leathem is Head, Catalog Department, Otto G. Richter Library, University of Miami, 1300 Memorial Drive, Coral Gables, FL 33124-0320 (E-mail: cleathem@miami.edu).

[Haworth co-indexing entry note]: "Choices in Cataloging Electronic Journals." Leathem, Cecilia A. Co-published simultaneously in *The Acquisitions Librarian* (The Haworth Information Press, an imprint of The Haworth Press, Inc.) No. 33/34, 2005, pp. 73-83; and: *Managing Digital Resources in Libraries* (ed: Audrey Fenner) The Haworth Information Press, an imprint of The Haworth Press, Inc., 2005, pp. 73-83. Single or multiple copies of this article are available for a fee from The Haworth Document Delivery Service [1-800-HAWORTH, 9:00 a.m. - 5:00 p.m. (EST). E-mail address: docdelivery@haworthpress.com].

Digital Object Identifier: 10.1300/J101v17n33_07

BACKGROUND

In a literature search for articles dealing with cataloging electronic journals, the author found that early concerns focused on the question: should the library catalog include bibliographic records for electronic journals and other online resources or is there a better way to provide information and access? OPACs (Online Public Access Catalogs) already had been widely adopted in libraries, but many of them were not Web-based and did not have the software to enable direct access to the online resource. Some libraries mounted lists of electronic journals and other resources and provided "hot links" on their own Web pages, thus providing direct access for their patrons and, in effect, bypassing the catalog. Users could locate and access electronic material on the Web site; however a researcher wishing to conduct a thorough search of all formats would need to perform a second search in the online catalog.

Often the lists were developed and maintained by librarians or staff outside the catalog department, typically by library systems personnel or reference staff. While the lists provided (and in many cases, continue to provide) simple access to the Web resources, they generally were little more than alphabetical arrangements by title. Still, this very simplicity has its supporters and one author observes that, "Even in print format, these users do not want to deal with catalog look-ups and call numbers. Beyond these observations, use data show . . . that Web lists work simply and simply work" (Chrzastowski, 320).

While well-maintained Web lists certainly provide ready, up-to-date access to online journals, the user will find they provide little or no descriptive information to assist in identifying appropriate material, and are not quick to address problems concerning title changes. Moreover, subject analysis is notable by its absence. As one writer states, "Web pages provide interesting and diverse types of user access, but no measure of management control, virtual or otherwise" (Hruska, 69).

Technical services librarians and serials catalogers in particular began to advocate the addition of full bibliographic records to describe and provide access to electronic journals via the library OPAC because, in the view of one author, they see the library catalog as a finding aid and not simply an inventory of items owned by the library (Morgan, 70). The need for subject analysis fuels another argument for full cataloging of these materials and one writer emphasizes the OPAC as the appropriate vehicle for providing subject access to electronic journals (Sleeman, 72).

For those catalogers and libraries committed to providing bibliographic records in the OPAC for electronic journals, a second question required an answer: How can we best accomplish this goal? Rare is the library without budget constraints for personnel and materials; rarer still is the catalog department that has not experienced staff cuts or shortages. Taking on the additional responsibility for cataloging electronic journals in straitened economic circumstances is daunting. Cataloging standards and policies for these materials, still in their infancy in the mid-1990s, were an additional complication for catalogers who would have to "learn as they go." Furthermore, librarians needed to develop some type of work-around if their OPAC used text-based and not Web-based software. The URL in the bibliographic record could provide access information but could not serve as a clickable link to the electronic resource. For fuller details and sources of information on these issues the reader may consult Ann W. Copeland's literature review published in *The Serials Librarian* (Copeland, 7-29) and Chaudhry's survey of current practices (Chaudhry, 434-443).

SINGLE RECORD vs. SEPARATE POLICY

Those librarians advocating catalog records for electronic journals must first consider the available resources they can use to keep up with the growing number of electronic journal titles. Given the budgetary and personnel constraints already discussed, most libraries are not able to provide additional support for cataloging electronic journals. Analysis of catalog department workflow and policies, together with an examination of the very nature of electronic resources are important activities that must predate the decision to begin cataloging. The fluid and sometimes transitory nature of electronic serial publications can affect decisions on their treatment. These publications have been described as differing from the more traditional print journals in several ways:

- They are not always issue-based and articles may be added over a period of time;
- Changes in volume and numbering are more common, or they may be dropped altogether;
- The Web site may change its name, location (such as the school, department or university sponsor), or address (French, 386).

SINGLE RECORD OPTION

Many libraries, assessing the volume of electronic journals available to them either by subscription, as part of a print plus electronic package deal with a publisher or a vendor, or freely accessed on the Web, make the decision to forgo preparing individual catalog records when they have cataloging copy for the print version. They opt instead to use an existing bibliographic record for the print version that already exists in the catalog and add information about the electronic journal. This decision is commonly known as the single record option.

According to CONSER Interim Guidelines, the single record must contain the 530 note field (for additional physical version) and the 856 field (to provide the URL and other location information). In addition, if the online title differs from the print version, a 730 or 740 field provides information and access via a title added entry (Hirons, 161).

Figure 1 illustrates the early practice of the Catalog Department, Otto G. Richter Library, when adding new electronic journals to the OPAC.

FIGURE 1. Single Record Option with MARC Tagging

001		32438440
005		19950510143553.0
008		950508c19959999dcuwr pbb 0 a0eng dnasKa
090		QD1|b.A4 Suppl
245	0 0	Journal of the American Chemical Society.|pSupporting information
246	1 0	Supporting information, journal of the American Chemical Society
260		[Washington, D.C.] :|bAmerican Chemical Society,|c1995-
300		v. ; 26 cm.
310		Weekly
362	0	Vol. 117, no. 5 (Feb. 8, 1995)-
515		Assumes vol. numbering of parent journal
530		Electronic version digitized and made available by the American Chemical Society
650	0	Chemistry|vPeriodicals
655	7	Internet resources|2local
655	7	Electronic journal|2local
710	2	American Chemical Society
780	0 0	|tJournal of the American Chemical Society. Supplementary material|w(OCoLC)4764975
856	4 1	|uhttp://pubs.acs.org/journals/jacsat/index.html|zOnline version [Access restricted to authorized UM patrons]

Note that the required 530 note field and 856 field containing the URL information are entered as prescribed, but other additional fields were deemed necessary to clarify the extent and source of the subscription. Information about the producer or provider of the online version is included in the 530 note and an added entry for the producer or publisher appears in the 710 added author field. Two local genre subject headings (655 fields) are added to provide subject access. The heading *Internet resources* is applied to every catalog record for electronic resources and the second heading *Electronic journal* is added to serials records. Figure 2 illustrates the public display of the single record option. In the Innovative Interfaces system used by Richter Library, the 856 field displays below the title and publication information as a hypertext link. The patron merely sees the link and any pertinent access restrictions that apply to the title, rather than the full URL.

FIGURE 2. Single Record Option–Public Display

Title	Journal of the American Chemical Society. Supporting information
Imprint	[Washington, D.C.] : American Chemical Society, 1995-

Connect to:
Online version
Access restricted to authorized UM faculty, staff, and students

Descript	v. : 26 cm.
Frequency	Weekly
Pub date	Vol. 117, no. 5 (Feb. 8, 1995)-
Note	Assumes vol. numbering of parent journal
	Electronic version digitized and made available by the American Chemical Society
Continues	Journal of the American Chemical Society. Supplementary material (OCoLC)4764975
Subject	Chemistry -- Periodicals
Genre	Internet resources
	Electronic journal
Alt author	American Chemical Society

Single Record Guidelines

While the single record option is a godsend to many libraries wishing to provide access through the OPAC, careful consideration is required before launching the cataloging effort. A CONSER Working Group provides specific guidance for the use of the single record and recommends its use in the following situations:

- Equivalent content
- The content of the paper and electronic version are the same but the titles differ
- The content is equivalent but the presentation differs (e.g., articles are added to an issue by the publisher as soon as they are ready, rather than releasing complete issue)
- The titles of the print and electronic versions change simultaneously
- GPO [i.e., Government Printing Office] single-record copy is available (*CONSER WG*)

The Library of Congress also provides criteria for deciding whether a single record approach is viable for a given journal title:

- Acquisitions/initial bibliographic control criterion. Does the degree of detail required for the management of initial and subsequent acquisitions actions require a separate record?
- Citation criterion. How much information is needed for a user to be able to get to the manifestation cited in the record? Is it clear to the user what is being cited?
- Interlibrary loan criterion. Will the receiver of a request know which manifestation is being requested and will the initiator of the request know which manifestations are available for loan?
- Bibliographic details criterion. Is it possible in a single record to indicate the significant bibliographic details of all of the manifestations cited in a record? (Hirons,162).

Single Record Approach: Advantages and Disadvantages

The single record approach has much to recommend it to librarians pressed for time and staffing. It is certainly much easier to make use of an existing record for the print version and add a few fields relating to the electronic version. Searching a bibliographic utility for appropriate cataloging copy, exporting a record to a local OPAC for editing, or creating original cataloging for each electronic journal is a time-consuming process. The single record approach, however, permits the library to provide access to a greater number of online journals in a shorter period. Since producers of electronic journals often issue individual articles online in advance of their publishing the full issue in print, a timely method of providing patrons access to the online version makes for good public service. Moreover, paraprofessional staff can be trained to edit existing records, thus freeing professionals for more complex cataloging activity. This makes good economic sense in many library environments.

Reference librarians also tend to prefer the single record approach; in their view, the patron enjoys "one-stop shopping" when they are able to find information about both the print and online holdings of a journal in one record. When all versions of a title are contained on a single bibliographic record, the patron always will be able to select the "correct" record.

There are drawbacks to the use of the single record approach. From a cataloging standpoint, the single record option does not provide full bibliographic description of the electronic version, but merely notes its existence and provides access information. In addition, bibliographic records for serials tend to be lengthy and adding additional fields to an existing record will increase its length and may necessitate a multiple screen or page display in the OPAC. When a library has access to an electronic journal through several host sites, the typical response is to add multiple URLs to the print record. The cataloger may also decide to add fields to display ISSN (International Standard Serial Number) for each available electronic version. Such long, complex records can create information overload and frustration for the library user.

Cooperative catalogs or consortia may experience problems when one library in the group has contractual access to an online journal but other libraries do not. If all the libraries add their holdings to one record, how do they indicate clearly that only one library provides access to the online version? In other OPACs, the user is able to limit searches by type of material; e.g., to limit their search only to the journal collection or only to online resources. As a result, a search may fail to pull up all journal titles if the user chooses to limit for online resources only. The cataloger needs to understand how their software works to determine if there is a way to work around the problem. At times, the software is not sophisticated enough to provide a viable solution.

Finally, the proliferation of vendor-supplied records may force libraries to reconsider the single record option. Some vendors offer free MARC records for the electronic journals they "bundle" for sale. Records for selected electronic journal collections are also available for purchase from a bibliographic utility, such as OCLC. A recent development is the service offered by vendors such as SerialsSolutions and TDNet who offer to supply full MARC records and regular updates for a library's electronic journal collection, including journals accessed via an aggregator database such as InfoTrac or WilsonWeb. When an aggregator or vendor adds or drops a title from the collection, libraries subscribing to one of the record services will receive updated tape loads that reflect the changes. Libraries using the single record option, however, will need to revisit and edit their records.

In order to achieve consistency, libraries adding vendor-supplied records also may wish to clean up their single records containing information about both the print and electronic versions of a journal. If they do not strip away the data for the electronic version, the patron will find one record in the OPAC describing the online version (with accompanying URLs) and another record describing the print version, but also containing information and a link to the electronic version. The potential for confusion on the part of the user is great.

SEPARATE RECORD OPTION

The decision to provide separate bibliographic records for print and electronic versions of a journal title is appealing because it provides a full cataloging description for each manifestation of the work. Each record is "cleaner" in that its focus is limited to describing one format and does not contain information on another version. While a title search will result in choice of records for the user, the more sophisticated software can provide visual assistance to aid in the proper record selection. In Figure 3, a search for the title, *Journal of the History of Ideas*, in the Richter Library online catalog results in a browse screen display. However, the software permits the use of icons to identify unambiguously the record for the electronic journal and assist the user's record selection.

Multiple Record Guidelines

There are occasions where a separate record must be created for the electronic version of a journal. CONSER recommends use of a separate record in the following instances:

- Resource exists only in electronic form
- Content of electronic resource differs significantly from print resource
- Resource undergoes a change in format, usually from print to electronic
- Resource is a database or Web site whose content is equivalent to more than one print source (e.g., Web of Science)
- Resource is a database or Web site whose content includes significant new material beyond existing print sources
- The original text cannot be definitely identified (*CONSER WG*)

Advantages and Disadvantages of the Separate Record

Libraries choosing to add separate records for each version of a journal believe that the benefits outweigh the costs of preparing cataloging copy in-house or using vendor-supplied copy. While the initial expense of using separate records is higher than that of choosing the single record option, database maintenance in the OPAC is much easier. If the library loses access rights to an online journal or if the Web site disappears, it is a simple matter to remove the record. It is faster, and thus cheaper, to delete records from the online catalog than it is to edit them. Libraries subscribing to vendor services which provide MARC records for titles in aggregator databases find that managing those records is a simple matter. The vendor will remove those titles no longer indexed in the aggregator database in the next update supplied to the library.

FIGURE 3. Browse Screen Display with Icons

Num	Mark	TITLES (1-2 of 2)	Medium	Year
Journal Of The History Of Ideas				
1	⌐	Journal Of The History Of Ideas		
		Richter Bound Periodicals, SpecFormat Film, Off-Campus Storage B1 .J75		
2	⌐	Journal Of The History Of Ideas [Electronic Resource]		
		INTERNET		

If a publisher ceases publishing the print version of a journal but maintains the electronic version, libraries using separate records can easily close the date and volume information on the print record while leaving the record for the electronic version intact. This obviates the need for complicated and messy notes that may serve to confuse the user. In a similar fashion, any variants in title or numbering that affect only one version can be reconciled more readily when separate records are in use.

The patron's needs also figure into the evaluation of the use of separate records. With more flexible software available to the library, allowing searches to be limited in scope and providing graphic clues to the format of the material, some argue that the user can be more self-sufficient and will require less library staff intervention. This is an important consideration for distance learners (Morris, 101). Morris and Allen further claim that they ". . . consider separate records to offer more clarity to users than single records. Users may well be presented with a choice of records, but at least when a record is selected all the information available is clear and concise . . ." (Morris, 100).

The primary disadvantages to providing separate records for print and electronic journals are the cost, time and effort expended in their initial creation. These considerations cannot be taken lightly in the current atmosphere of fiscal constraint. As the library's collection of electronic journals grows, staff allocated to providing separate records inevitably will be diverted from treating other materials unless the library is in the fortunate position of hiring new staff.

There also exists the potential for failed searches, especially as users act on their increasing preference for online, full-text material. If the user limits the search to electronic resources in the OPAC, he will not find print-only journals. This may or may not present a problem when the search is for a known title, but certainly will affect the results obtained from subject searches.

A CONSER report describes another problem that may arise when two versions of the same title are widely separated in the browse display, ". . . particularly if there are many monographs with the same title filed between them, e.g., Blood [a serial]. Blood [twelve monographs by that name], Blood (Online)" (*CONSER WG*).

CONCLUSION

When debating the cataloging options for electronic journals, each library must decide how best to deploy scarce resources in their local environment and meet basic public service requirements. In the author's library, the initial decision was to use the single record option whenever feasible to catalog electronic journals that were also held in print format. Improvements in the OPAC software and the advent of vendor-supplied MARC records for journal collections and for titles held in aggregator databases have led to a change in favor of separate records for the print and electronic versions. At this time, the separate record option appears to allow the library to take advantage of services and products that are currently available and to have the flexibility to accommodate future commercial developments.

REFERENCES

Chaudhry, Abdus S. and Makeswary Periasamy. "A Study of Current Practices of Selected Libraries in Cataloguing Electronic Journals." *Library Review (Glasgow, Scotland)* 50 (2001): 434-443.

Chrzastowski, Tina E. "E-Journal Access: The Online Catalog (856 field), Web Lists, and 'The Principle of Least Effort' at the Chemistry Library, University of Illinois." *Library Computing* 18 (1999): 320. ProQuest. Otto G. Richter Library. 23 Apr. 2003 <http://proquest.umi.com/>.

CONSER WG: Single v. Separate Records. Draft Report. 1999. 29 Mar. 2003 <http://wwwtest.library.ucla.edu/libraries/cataloging/sercat/conserwg/conserwg.draft.htm#top>.

Copeland, Ann W. "E-Serials Cataloging in the 1990s: A Review of the Literature." *The Serials Librarian* 41.3/4 (2002): 7-29.

French, Patricia S. "Cataloging Electronic Serials. Report of a Workshop at the 1997 NASIG Conference." *The Serials Librarian* 34.3/4 (1998): 385-389.

Hirons, Jean. "The Interim Guidelines for Online Versions." *The Serials Librarian* 34.1/2 (1998): 159-164.

Hruska, Martha. "Remote Internet Serials in the OPAC?" *Serials Review* 21.4 (1995): 68-70.

Morgan, Eric Lease. "Adding Internet Resources to our OPACs." *Serials Review* 21.4 (1995): 70-72.

Morris, Wayne and Lynda Thomas. "Single or Separate OPAC Records for E-Journals: The Glamorgan Perspective." *The Serials Librarian* 28.3/4 (1996): 97-109.

Sleeman, Allison Mook. "Cataloging Remote Access Electronic Materials." *Serials Review* 21.4 (1995): 72.

ELIN@:
Electronic Library Information Navigator–
Towards the "One Stop Shop"

Anna Alwerud
Lotte Jorgensen

SUMMARY. Libraries subscribe to thousands of electronic journals and they are difficult for end-users to find. Journal and publisher interfaces and functionalities differ considerably. The recent development in e-media calls for central management of the resources. Lund University Libraries' Head Office has developed a service for presentation and administration of e-journals, ELIN@. The service is used by ten Swedish academic libraries. This article describes the ELIN@ user interface and the administration tool. ELIN@ offers a "one stop shop" that makes e-journals searchable on an article level in one single interface together with other selected material, e.g., e-print archives. Personalisation and easy ordering are other user facilities. The consistent statistics obtained in ELIN@ provide administrators with tools for selection and acquisition, and library branding puts the quality stamp on the material that users and funding agencies need. *[Article copies available for a fee from The Haworth Document Delivery Service: 1-800-HAWORTH. E-mail address: <docdelivery@haworthpress.com> Website: <http://www.HaworthPress.com> © 2005 by The Haworth Press, Inc. All rights reserved.]*

Anna Alwerud is Librarian, Lund University Libraries Head Office, Box 134, SE-221 00 Lund, Sweden (E-mail: anna.alwerud@lub.lu.se). Lotte Jorgensen is Librarian, Lund University Libraries Head Office, Box 134, SE-221 00 Lund, Sweden (E-mail: lotte.jorgensen@lub.lu.se).

[Haworth co-indexing entry note]: "ELIN@: Electronic Library Information Navigator–Towards the 'One Stop Shop.'" Alwerud, Anna, and Lotte Jorgensen. Co-published simultaneously in *The Acquisitions Librarian* (The Haworth Information Press, an imprint of The Haworth Press, Inc.) No. 33/34, 2005, pp. 85-95; and: *Managing Digital Resources in Libraries* (ed: Audrey Fenner) The Haworth Information Press, an imprint of The Haworth Press, Inc., 2005, pp. 85-95. Single or multiple copies of this article are available for a fee from The Haworth Document Delivery Service [1-800-HAWORTH, 9:00 a.m. - 5:00 p.m. (EST). E-mail address: docdelivery@haworthpress.com].

http://www.haworthpress.com/web/AL
© 2005 by The Haworth Press, Inc. All rights reserved.
Digital Object Identifier: 10.1300/J101v17n33_08

KEYWORDS. Libraries, electronic journals, electronic resources, management, statistics, user interface, collection management

BACKGROUND

Lund University (LU), situated in the south of Sweden, is the country's largest institution for research and higher education. LU has 24,000 FTEs that multiply into 35,000 individuals because many of the students attend part-time courses. In addition there are around 6,000 researchers and staff. LU has four smaller branches located in other cities in the region. The university is divided into the following faculties:

- Technology
- Natural sciences
- Law
- Economics, social and political science
- Medicine
- Humanities
- Music, theatre and the arts

The multidisciplinary character of the university is obvious. Research and education are carried out in virtually all subjects. Library service is provided at present by seventeen faculty or department libraries organized in a network (Lund University Libraries, http://www.lub.lu.se/) coordinated by the Library Head Office with main responsibilities for policy issues, quality control and the University Electronic Library, including electronic publishing initiatives and strategies for Lund University.

The certification of the network libraries indicates that they fulfill certain statutory criteria of professional services. The Library Board determines these criteria. In addition to the network libraries, there are numerous smaller institutional libraries with varying service standards.

During the last few years significant changes have taken place in the general service ambition: end-user orientation is one and the increasing supply of electronic media the other. Libraries have become more student oriented, while at the same time maintaining a high level of service for researchers. A certified network library is required to have special facilities for students. Two faculties are currently developing learning resource centers for students.

The launch of the decentralised network library organisation coincided with the boom in electronic media. While the network libraries took over responsibilities such as cataloguing, interlibrary loans and user training from the main library, it became obvious that central management of the electronic resources was necessary. The Head Office includes departments responsible for operating and maintaining the library OPAC, for managing and developing the electronic library services including licensing of databases and electronic media, for electronic publishing, for knowledge technologies and distant learning, and for a media department offering repro services, scanning, digitizing, etc.

Prioritized areas of development are to refine and develop the infrastructure, mechanisms and technologies that have been created for the Lund University Electronic Thesis and Dissertation service, and to offer the university a complete system, the ELIN@ service–Electronic Library Information Navigator. ELIN@ gives our end-users a single point of access to a wide variety of licensed journals, databases and open archives and at the same time offers the library staff easy administration tools for managing electronic content.

Via agreements with a very large number of publishers and other information providers, the ELIN@ service has acquired metadata of +12,000.000 records (April 2003) and made them searchable and retrievable on document level in one single user interface, with cross searching, merged search results and many more advantages for end users. Experiences from the nine other university libraries in Sweden clearly show a significant increase of the usage of the information resources (journals, databases, open archives, etc.) included in the ELIN@ service. New content is added continuously. ELIN@ offers alert services (Table of Contents alerts and SDI-alerts), integration with reference management tools, etc.

ELIN@ was launched in 2001 and ten academic institutions in Sweden are now using ELIN@. This article describes the ELIN@ user interface and the administration tool, and explains our reasons for creating a system like ELIN@.

WHY ELIN@?

There are thousands of e-journals and they are often difficult for end-users to find. Journal interfaces and functionalities differ considerably. One of the problems with the many different user interfaces is that the average end-user has no knowledge of the publishing world, journals change publishers, journal titles change and so forth. ELIN@ was created to give them a "one stop shop" (About ELIN@, http://pluto.lub. lu.se/about/one.html).

We also wanted to avoid the "publisher trap," i.e., the presentation of e-journals in separate publisher databases, a system very confusing for end-users and one that significantly restricts their overview of the library's total collection of e-media. (See Figure 1.)

Another reason was the need for library branding. Probably most librarians are familiar with the question "What do we need the library for when we can find all information for free on the Internet?" Most users are not aware that probably the majority of the full-text articles they download "for free" come from fee-based journals paid for by the library. Some publishers give libraries the possibility of having their institution's name or even a logo somewhere on the publisher's home page/user interface. If there is a library name it is often in very small font, chosen by the publisher and easily overlooked. Consistent branding of the library is very important for many reasons. Fund givers need to know that they get value for money, and researchers and students must have confidence in the library's collections: branding is the "quality stamp" of the library.

The traditional pattern of research publishing is changing. Important research is now often published in preprint archives or in open archives. One of the main reasons for creating ELIN@ was the need to integrate this kind of open access information into the electronic library.

THE USER INTERFACE AND FUNCTIONALITIES OF ELIN@

Our main objective for the user interface was to "keep it simple" and present the results fast.

What did we want from the interface?

Cross searching different article types. (See Figure 2.)

Three search options are offered: Simple, Basic and Advanced with Common Command Language search. In the basic search you can do word and phrase searches combined with Boolean operators and truncation. You can search specific collections and publication years and limit the search to documents available in full text. If the search result exceeds twenty hits the refine option appears.

The search fields are: All fields, Article title, Author name, Journal title, ISSN, Abstract, and Keywords. The search results are presented as a

FIGURE 1

FIGURE 2

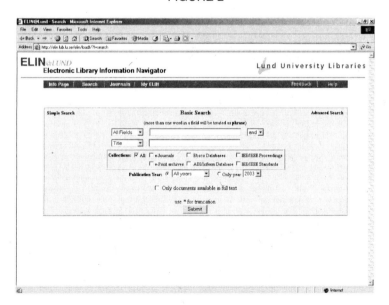

list with basic bibliographic information and links to abstracts with full document information and links to the full text. On the full document information page is a link to the table of contents (TOC) of the issue the article is part of and an option to export the reference to a reference management program.

The e-mail alert options for both Selective Dissemination of Information and TOCs are highly used. We are planning to introduce more functionalities in the personalized My ELIN, e.g., links to reference works, messages from Your Librarian, and a bookmark collection all based on subject areas. (See Figure 3.)

As we wanted to avoid password administration we are using the central LDAP university staff database for access control for the personalized functions and for remote access. Journal titles can be listed based on search, browsed alphabetically, and browsed by subject, i.e., you can find a journal title based on a reference, or starting with a specific letter, or get an overview of journal titles within a specific subject area. (See Figure 4.)

All articles not available in full text can be ordered through a central ordering system. If the user has chosen the personal login version My ELIN@, the necessary personal information about the user is automati-

FIGURE 3

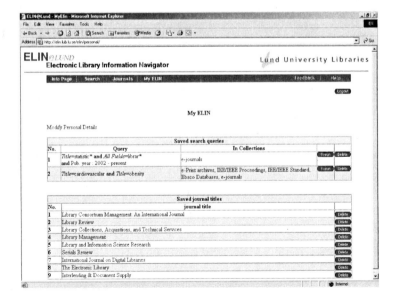

FIGURE 4

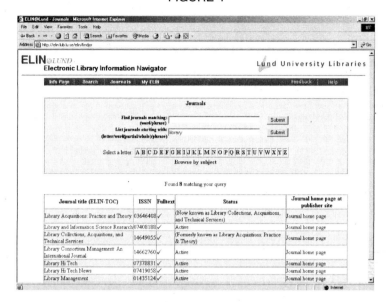

cally filled in on the order form as well as the bibliographic article information. (See Figure 5.)

THE ADMINISTRATIVE TOOL

Through the administrative tool library staff can add and remove titles and browse titles based on metadata provider, publisher, title, and ISSN. It is possible to import and export files. (See Figure 6.)

The statistics function gives the library first-hand knowledge of how journal titles are used and thus we are not depending on undocumented usage data from publishers or no data at all. Usage statistics are sorted on institutional and faculty levels. At present the information we get is the number of full text retrievals and the number of TOCs per journal title. We plan to develop a more sophisticated statistics tool. Reliable usage statistics make for better collection management and might facilitate a shift from package deals back to selection, possibly resulting in better economy and freeing us from being at the mercy of the large publishers. (See Figure 7.)

Logging tells us about the use of functions and what we need to teach the users. With refined administrative tools, subject specialists within

FIGURE 5

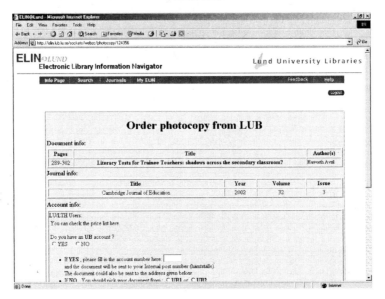

FIGURE 6

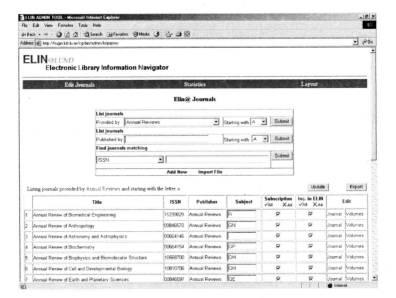

FIGURE 7

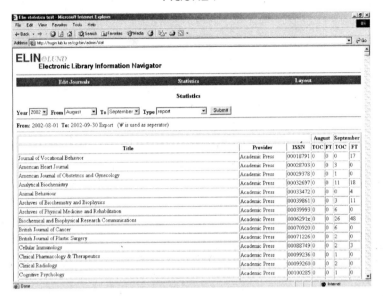

the library network will be provided with reports and could be directly involved in the presentation and selection of resources and in the administration (where suitable). In this way ELIN@ will not only be a centrally-run service but will also engage and use all staff in an efficient way.

Through the administrative tool, different institutions using ELIN@ can customise and change the layout of their own ELIN@ interface. (See Figure 8.)

ADVANTAGES OF ELIN@

End-users need to know only one single user interface to search all e-journals independent of publisher or provider platform. Material from all publishers is cross-searched simultaneously. Libraries do not need to spend time training their end-users in different user interfaces. The librarian only has to say "check in ELIN@." The end-user does not need to know the publisher of a journal title or which library is buying it as all titles are presented in one list. Other material types such as e-prints, standards, conference proceedings, and aggregated databases are included in ELIN@ and are cross-searched together with the e-journals.

FIGURE 8

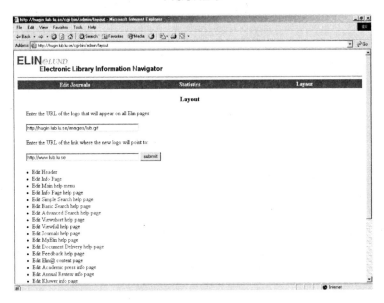

The feedback function gives us immediate information about problems. Because we control ELIN@ we can act upon problems fast, for example, by adding information to the help text directly. Suggestions from users can be implemented fast, and so forth.

Our main ambition is for the material bought by the library to be used. We can see from the usage statistics that as soon as a publisher is added to ELIN@ the usage is rising. This means that publishers have a decided interest in including their titles in ELIN@ because this will increase the visibility of their portfolio and reduce the risk of cancellations.

The fact that the library controls ELIN@ is very attractive: We decide how it looks, we decide what is included and what is not, we decide which functionalities we want to develop. If the system is slowing down because of high usage it is up to us to solve the problem. We are not depending on others to make the decisions and it gives us the possibility of serving our users, both libraries and end-users, in a much more flexible and cost-effective manner than if we had depended on either the services provided by publishers or by subscription agents.

APPENDIX: ELIN@ Content

Publisher data
Wiley & Sons 430 journals
Blackwell Publishing 570 journals
Taylor & Francis 740 journals
Annual Reviews 29 journals
Springer 403 journals
Emerald (MCB University Press) 139 journals
Institute of Physics (IOP) 37 journals
Karger 81 journals
Elsevier (ScienceDirect) 1300 journals
Academic Press 341 journals
Kluwer 758 journals
Project Muse 180 journals
IEE/IEEE 165 journals + proceedings + standards
BioMed Central 55 Journals

E-print and pre-print archives
arXiv (Los Alamos)
Cogprints
Caltech's Electronic Theses and Dissertations
University of Duisburg Electronic Theses and Dissertations

Aggregated databases
Business Source Elite EBSCO
Academic Search Elite EBSCO
ABI Inform ProQuest

Table of Contents data
ETOCs from British Library

Western Michigan University Libraries' "Electronic Journal Finder"

Randle Gedeon
George Boston

SUMMARY. This article describes the development of the "Electronic Journal Finder," a TDNet installation for the University Libraries of Western Michigan University. Topics covered include: rationale for subscription, project timeline, content, product customization, set-up, maintenance issues, reporting functions, directing URL links, searching utility, level of acceptance, product functionality, and conclusions. *[Article copies available for a fee from The Haworth Document Delivery Service: 1-800-HAWORTH. E-mail address: <docdelivery@haworthpress.com> Website: <http://www.HaworthPress.com> © 2005 by The Haworth Press, Inc. All rights reserved.]*

KEYWORDS. Academic libraries, aggregating services, electronic journal management, electronic journals, TDNet, Western Michigan University libraries

---

Randle Gedeon is Assistant Head, Acquisitions and Serials Resources Department, Waldo Library, Western Michigan University, 1903 West Michigan Avenue, Kalamazoo, MI 49008-5353 (E-mail: randle.gedeon@wmich.edu). George Boston is Electronic Resources Specialist, Serials Resources Department, Waldo Library, Western Michigan University, 1903 West Michigan Avenue, Kalamazoo, MI 49008-5353 (E-mail: george.boston@wmich.edu).

[Haworth co-indexing entry note]: "Western Michigan University Libraries' 'Electronic Journal Finder.'" Gedeon, Randle, and George Boston. Co-published simultaneously in *The Acquisitions Librarian* (The Haworth Information Press, an imprint of The Haworth Press, Inc.) No. 33/34, 2005, pp. 97-106; and: *Managing Digital Resources in Libraries* (ed: Audrey Fenner) The Haworth Information Press, an imprint of The Haworth Press, Inc., 2005, pp. 97-106. Single or multiple copies of this article are available for a fee from The Haworth Document Delivery Service [1-800-HAWORTH, 9:00 a.m. - 5:00 p.m. (EST). E-mail address: docdelivery@haworthpress.com].

Digital Object Identifier: 10.1300/J101v17n33_09

INTRODUCTION

Like many other academic libraries, the University Libraries of Western Michigan University started delving heavily into electronic serials in 1997 and 1998. Patron access was provided largely through the Libraries' home page via a large, segmented alphabetical list containing at its height over 2,000 titles. The shortcomings of this approach were numerous: (1) it was quite labor intensive to maintain; every bit of data had to be fed into it; (2) it was not dynamically updated, requiring constant attention; (3) the library was wrestling with what content to include; and (4) the integrated titles found in aggregated databases were excluded, for it just was not practical to enter that jungle without powerful outside serials management software. The library operated with the clunky alphabetical list since 1997, all the while watching our e-journal offerings grow exponentially. Something had to be done.

Timeline

By the spring of 2001, strong consideration was being given to the purchase of e-serials management software with a view to making a decision by fall of that year. Discussions wrapped up by fall with a commitment to purchase TDNet hosted software that November. The setup period consumed most of the spring and by the end of April the installation was operational for the staff to start whipping it into shape. The prototype was available summer 2002 for our public services staff to begin familiarizing themselves with it. The site went live in August 2002.

EJF FULL-TEXT CONTENT

The library's TDNet installation, named the "Electronic Journal Finder," provides access to approximately 13,700 electronic journals; 11,000 constitute unique titles, along with approximately 2,700 individually cataloged titles. University Libraries subscribe to an array of publishers' e-journal collections including: the ACM Digital Library, ACS Web Editions, AMS Journal Search, American Institute of Physics, Emerald Fulltext, Highwire Press, IEEE Xplore, JSTOR, Ovid Nursing Collection, Project Muse, ScienceDirect, and SIAM Journals.

CUSTOMIZATION

A small team of three public service librarians and the two acquisitions/serials librarians customized parts of the front end of our installation (www.tdnet.com/wmu/). The color scheme, banners, and some buttons were altered. Blue was chosen as a background color; the banner is similar to the library homepage; and three buttons were added–the first linking to the OPAC, and the other two linking to in-house authored help screens, and information about our subscribed e-journal collections. (See Figure 1.)

The help screens (www.wmich.edu/library/ej/help.html) provide explanatory text detailing the ways to search the EJF (Quick Search, Alphabetical List, and TDNet Search), the different ways the EJF may connect to an article (directly linking to the journal or linking to the database), advice for searching within databases, and an explanation of the results screen. (See Figure 2.)

Search results are displayed in the following order: (1) the journal title, (2) the service providing the journal, (3) the dates of online coverage, (4) whether print or microfilm holdings exist at WMU, and (5) table of contents information (if it exists).

Information Icons

Informative notes can be placed within an icon attached to an entry. These notes are created through the administrative module and may apply to specific titles or to all the titles in a service or to all the titles from a publisher. Most of our notes are fairly simple, offering search tips applicable to given services, and providing researchers with clues as to what they might hope to find. The library has not kept statistics on the use of these notes, but there is some assurance for the library staff in knowing that they exist for our patrons.

DATA SET-UP

Three main lists were drawn up in Excel and forwarded to TDNet: List #1 detailed the contents of aggregated collections where access is available to all titles held in a collection, e.g., JSTOR, Project Muse, and Emerald. List #2 detailed individual e-journal titles within packages where the library has access to only a percentage, e.g., American Physi-

FIGURE 1. The Electronic Journal Finder, University Libraries, Western Michigan University

FIGURE 2. EJF Results Explanation

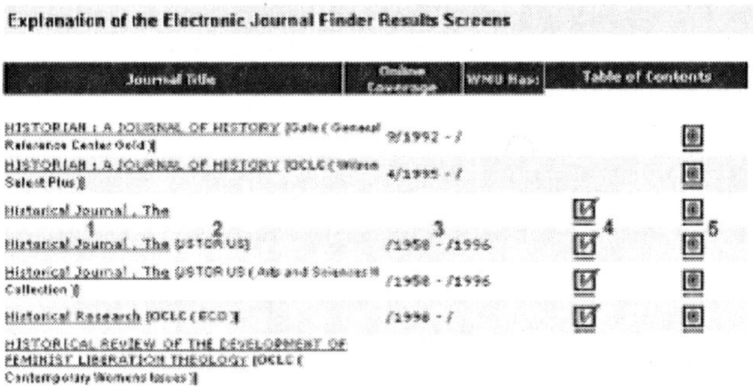

cal Society, Highwire Press, and Kluwer Online; and, List #3 detailed aggregated databases with full-text content, e.g., InfoTrac Databases, Lexis-Nexis, and Newsbank Newspapers. An additional file containing our print ISSN equivalents was also sent, allowing for a link between TDNet and our library's integrated system, Endeavor's Voyager. Once these files are integrated the basic content of the service is present. Also sent were image files defining banners, buttons and the HTML behind them.

Set-Up Form

The library submitted the TDNet form providing contact information, designated options for hosting and document delivery, IP authorization, proxy server information, Z39.50 link structure, TDNet data files for catalog, data file structure and format, site customization, and title lists.

MAINTENANCE ISSUES (DURING SET-UP)

All of the content was entered by late June 2002, beginning a period of product refinement lasting about two months. This refinement involved discerning how all the aggregating services interface with TDNet. Potentially, separate issues exist for each service used. Some links set up correctly, but others were problematic, e.g., several InfoTrac databases linked to the basic menu page (InfoTrac) and not the designated database. All of the aggregator content had to be checked, revealing similar problems within services. Twelve to fifteen randomly selected titles from each service were checked, revealing problems or patterns if they were there to be found. Link status was confirmed by mousing over the status bar revealing the URL for a visual check of appropriateness. This process speeds up as the investigator gains experience with what the URLs should look like. Individually subscribed e-journals were subjected to a link-by-link confirmation establishing that the links were reaching the correct destination. Two staff members and an experienced student worker performed these checks.

Maintenance Issues (While Up and Running)

TDNet advertises weekly updates; though perhaps technically true, we have found that in practice the updates are bi-weekly. The files are updated the following Monday, if the requests are submitted Tuesday the week before. Every week something is found by the library requiring an update to the EJF. It may take the form of new e-journal subscriptions, additional e-journal packages, or just the modification of existing content. Changes are effected through the administrative module, which permits multiple simultaneous users logged on with the same username and password. This is helpful for e-serial administrators and staff keeping current with subscriptions and making changes, which is a routine occurrence particularly with e-titles received free with print subscriptions. The process is very straightforward and easily enough done if the servers are responsive. It bears mentioning that we are constantly checking links and making sure that they are going to the appropriate site, even after subscribing to this service.

Maintenance Issues (General Observations)

Global changes by TDNet occur rarely, sometimes resulting in the loss of our customized URL links. Also, we have noticed that in some cases TDNet treats dynamic URLs like static URLs. Both situations require regular checking of the database. Server slowness is sometimes a problem, particularly toward the afternoon after 11:00 A.M. EST. when a few West Coast clients come online. Server traffic is first directed to Europe, perhaps leading to additional slowness. There is more ongoing maintenance required than just "set up and forget it," which is how we originally (and surely idealistically) envisioned the product.

Maintenance Issues (Non-TDNet)

The TDNet service links to content; there is no subscription management. Differing services often translate into differing nuances; with growth, expansion and mergers, there are now perhaps up to one hundred different services to track with differing payment practices, potentially impacting cost and assigned URLs. Status changes are not obvious through TDNet and patrons are denied access to particular titles when problematic titles slip through. Checking links manually is still the only way to know for certain that they are correct.

HANDLING MAJOR PACKAGES

TDNet handles the updating of major e-journal collections quite well. Almost all titles are updated automatically with little difficulty, perhaps reflecting upon the type of files provided by the various services to TDNet. Once in a while, prior titles are missed. These updates occur as a matter of course and no alerts are offered, so e-resource personnel need to be aware that the files are regularly being updated. Our subscribed e-journal collection contains approximately 2,800 titles from journal packages. Of those, around seventy percent (1,900) fall into the automatically updated category. The other thirty percent are dealt with individually in the administrative module.

Programming

TDNet is an Israeli company and most of the programming is done in Israel, potentially impacting the speed of commerce. Inquiries are sent to a domestic contact, who often filters our questions through to the programmers in Israel. The basic software has been upgraded since Waldo Library began using the service.

REPORTS

The statistics report generator, found in the administrative module, allows for customized statistical reports defined by type. The report generator offers a great many search parameters, perhaps too many. Most small reports are produced immediately, while summary reports can run very slowly. When summary reports are ordered, all titles in the database are put through the system one by one. Consequently, this type of report takes some time to download. It is clearly our perception that the system gathers many differing types of data, which is true enough, but the journals must be used to make their way into a report. At the time of writing, 6,000 of the 13,000 unique titles in our database had been accessed at least once. As use goes up, so goes the worth of the reporting function; use to date has not constituted enough to really build up convincing reports. Ultimately these reports will provide us with a great deal of comparative data. TDNet does not offer the ability to automatically replicate reports on a weekly, monthly, quarterly, etc., basis, so any report requires an overt request. Keep in mind that these reports detail e-journal use through the EJF only, not for access through bookmarked sites or through our library's OPAC.

CONTENTS

Essentially, the EJF is a sophisticated link manager affording significant functionality including the ability to search for particular titles, browse lists of e-journals, configure usage reports, run searches and sorts on the database content. Our customized screen contains columnar data for journal title, dates of coverage, links to our OPAC, and some tables of contents, which represents a leaner, scaled-down version of the default model proposed by TDNet. The constituent elements of a given listing may vary. Not many listings have tables of contents, where all of our subscribed titles link to our OPAC and have TOC listings. The catalog links are keyed to ISSN; if the e-version does not have a separate ISSN, sub-field "a" from field 022 of the print record displays.

Determining Where the Links Go

Where the link connects the user is dictated by database capability. Not all of our listings have title-level links, so where Gale databases link to the article level, all OCLC databases (excluding ECO) go to a database access page, ProQuest has journal-level links, and Lexis-Nexis listings link to a searching interface. TDNet has a handle on these capabilities and most links go to the article or journal-level link, with only a few problematic ones causing trouble.

What Is Not Included?

Our library chose to exclude indexing databases and chose not to list our print holdings. Clearly other institutions include this content; adding the print holdings offers patrons the equivalent of a serials shelf list, potentially a nice bonus. However, we felt that including these options would entail much additional maintenance and our thinking was that many indexing databases already link to journals and, if included, our product would no longer technically be the "Electronic Journal Finder."

LIMITED SEARCHING UTILITY

Each connection to an e-journal or aggregated collection opens a new window and patrons are encouraged to close windows as they go along, which can prove to be bothersome. Buttons along the top take the user to that given page. The "Quick Search" option offers a left-anchored key phrase, searching in the title, publisher, ISSN, or vendor fields. Searching by publisher, ISSN, or vendor are good options for staff, but not many patrons find these fields relevant to their needs. Regular searching options are buried several layers within the EJF and offer questionable subject analytics. Keyword searching is an equivalent to ad-hoc subject searching. For instance, a search for "chemistry" nets sixty-eight records containing chemistry somewhere in the title.

Listings are occasionally presented in a confounding manner. Many journal titles begin with a numeral or a date, and titles in these categories are not found using a letter-designated button. Lists are ASCII sorted, not numerically sorted, further complicating matters. Abbreviations appear out of alphabetical order and the lack of or presence of a period can change the location of a title within a list. All of this raises the question, how does the patron search?

LEVEL OF ACCEPTANCE

Despite these shortcomings, the EJF has started gaining stature in our library system as a valuable tool for the serious researcher. Public service librarians regularly refer patrons to the EJF when citations are known. Patrons are encouraged to search by the journal title or ISSN if known. The EJF is often mentioned and sometimes taught in graduate and upper-level undergraduate bibliographic instruction sessions, with students and faculty expressing delight at its presence. It is not being taught in BI sessions for lower-level undergraduates, where only the basics are covered and where it is felt that the standard fifty-minute session affords too little time. Additionally, it is felt that these students should be encouraged to first direct their research efforts into indexing and abstracting databases, rather than go trolling for relevant-sounding full-text articles.

FUNCTIONALITY

The EJF can be searched by title and has replaced our clunky alphabetic list with a greatly expanded version, updating quantities of data that we could not possibly keep up with, given our present staffing situation. It saves a lot of electronic serials work.

CONCLUSIONS

This project involved more setup on our behalf than we first realized, developing a deep appreciation for the complexity involved in dealing with resources held within aggregated databases. Refining linkages and URLs was a big project; we had a high and sophisticated set of expectations but found many inaccurate matches. There was a learning curve for us dealing with this kind of data and TDNet was a relatively new company at the time. It is fair to say that we learned together, benefiting future client institutions and their patrons through our experiences.

Postscript

Since this article was accepted for publication, TDNet has announced an interface software upgrade to Version 1.10 effecting display and searching capabilities and providing further customization and enhancement features.

Integrating Print and Electronic Resources: Joyner Library's "Pirate Source"

Clark Nall

Janice Steed Lewis

SUMMARY. Valuable information in print is often neglected because of the rapid proliferation of electronic resources and the bias of many library users against print sources. At Joyner Library, it was decided to construct an interactive subject guide database that included resources in all formats to offer users a convenient starting point for research and to encourage use of neglected resources. The resulting database is called Pirate Source <http://systems.lib.ecu.edu/piratesource/> and is designed to allow flexibility in the addition of subject areas and resources by multiple contributors. In Pirate Source, the user can limit results according to the type of information sought and by online and in-library resources. The database has proven successful with the user population and library personnel, and is heavily used by patrons, at public service desks, and in bibliographic instruction. *[Article copies available for a fee from The Haworth Document Delivery Service: 1-800-HAWORTH. E-mail address: <docdelivery@haworthpress.com> Website: <http://www.HaworthPress.com> © 2005 by The Haworth Press, Inc. All rights reserved.]*

Clark Nall is Instruction/Reference Librarian, Joyner Library, East Carolina University, Greenville, NC 27858-4353 (E-mail: nallh@mail.ecu.edu). Janice Steed Lewis is Interim Head of Reference, Joyner Library, East Carolina University, Greenville, NC 27858-4353 (E-mail: lewisja@mail.ecu.edu).

[Haworth co-indexing entry note]: "Integrating Print and Electronic Resources: Joyner Library's 'Pirate Source.'" Nall, Clark, and Janice Steed Lewis. Co-published simultaneously in *The Acquisitions Librarian* (The Haworth Information Press, an imprint of The Haworth Press, Inc.) No. 33/34, 2005, pp. 107-120; and: *Managing Digital Resources in Libraries* (ed: Audrey Fenner) The Haworth Information Press, an imprint of The Haworth Press, Inc., 2005, pp. 107-120. Single or multiple copies of this article are available for a fee from The Haworth Document Delivery Service [1-800-HAWORTH, 9:00 a.m. - 5:00 p.m. (EST). E-mail address: docdelivery@haworthpress.com].

KEYWORDS. Database-driven Web site, interactive subject guide, Pirate Source, reference services, Web site design

Integration of print and electronic resources is an ongoing challenge for today's librarian. Many students and librarians prefer the convenience of querying a database for information or scanning online sources rather than facing the perceived difficulties and time involved in identifying, locating and using a print source. Library instruction sessions often focus on online searching techniques and methods of accessing electronic resources to the near exclusion of print sources.

In early 2002, librarians at Joyner Library at East Carolina University decided that the pendulum had swung too far in favor of electronic resources. We were evaluating, ordering, cataloging and shelving wonderful subject encyclopedias, bibliographies, directories, and other reference materials, but they were receiving very little use. Many of these materials were included on our print and Web-based subject guides, but with time constraints, staff turnover, and other pressures, the subject guides were not always kept up-to-date. In many cases, an important print resource or database was appropriate for inclusion on several subject guides. When we received a new edition, a Web address changed, a subscription was canceled, or other changes occurred, each subject guide had to be modified individually.

How could we better integrate print sources into our library instruction sessions, familiarize users with recommended print reference materials, and decrease the time required to maintain subject guides? A database-driven Web site for our subject guides seemed to be the answer.

Literature and Web searches found several successful examples of database-driven sites in use in libraries. Gary Roberts described the design process for the InfoIguana ready reference database at Alfred University's Herrick Library. Herrick Library faced some of the same concerns we did in designing and defining the database. These included:

- articulating a role for the database separate from that of the library online public access catalog (OPAC)
- incorporating active searching behaviors by the user rather than simply offering a "canned" browsable page
- minimizing creation and maintenance time
- developing an input screen that did not require extensive HTML coding skills (Roberts, 28 and 30).

Librarians at Herrick Library believed that InfoIguana would provide a more focused scope than the OPAC, help inexperienced users who wanted to quickly locate the core resources in a specific subject area, and incorporate Web-based resources not in their OPAC. They concluded that their "OPAC already answers the need for a comprehensive catalog of our physical collection. The ready-reference database would clearly fill a different need" (Roberts, 30). They used Active Server Pages and Microsoft Access to create a dynamic database that incorporated active searching behavior by users. A simple input screen decreased creation and maintenance time (Roberts, 30).

While Herrick Library's experience was very beneficial to us as we designed our database, we also incorporated ideas gleaned from Web pages and databases at a number of other academic libraries, including Virginia Military Institute's SourceFinder <http://www.vmi.edu/sourcefinder/>, California Polytechnic State University's DataGenie <http://www.lib.calpoly.edu/research/data_genie.html>, and the Info-Dome at Lehigh University <http://www.lehigh.edu/library/infodome/infodome.html>.

DATABASE DESIGN

The reference department took a lead role in defining the organization and structure of the database. In a series of brainstorming sessions, we considered a variety of possible features and structures for the database. Consensus was reached on these points:

- We would try to seamlessly integrate print, microform, subscription databases, CD-ROM sources and high-quality, carefully selected free Web sites within the database so that the user would be presented with a variety of choices based on content, rather than format.
- At the same time, users would have the option to limit to Web-based or in-library items. This option was important since the university was in the process of expanding its distance education program. Plus, many students in traditional classes preferred the convenience of accessing materials from dormitory rooms or their homes.
- Subjects would conform to the names of academic departments and schools at East Carolina University when possible. We felt that this would help undergraduates select the correct subject area.

- Source types could vary according to the subject, i.e., "Dictionaries" could be used for one subject, while "Dictionaries & Encyclopedias" might be used for a different subject that might have fewer resources of these types or where "encyclopedic dictionaries" predominated.
- We would be able to prioritize the way items displayed on the retrieval list. For example, PsycInfo might be the first item to display in a search for Psychology–Find Articles, even though other databases preceded it alphabetically. We did this by including a ranking option on the data entry form. The default ranking was "100," meaning that all items within a source type for a subject would be ranked alphabetically. A ranking of "1" could be used for as many items as desired. The items ranked "1" would sort alphabetically, followed by the items ranked "100."
- Each entry would include a brief description of the resource. Users could decide whether or not to display all the descriptions. If a user chose not to display all the descriptions on the initial result screen, there would still be an option from the result list to see the description of a specific item.

We were able to include all these features in the first iteration of the database. In retrospect, conforming our subject heading to the academic structure was probably less important than we initially thought. Many freshman English students, for example, write research papers on topics of their choice, which can range from the death penalty to health care reform. Obviously, the "English" subject could not be broad enough to include all the recommended sources for researching these types of topics. Moreover, we quickly added other subjects to the database, such as "Career Research" (a popular paper topic), "Images & Clip Art," and "Law." Almost as quickly, we realized that broad subject areas needed to be divided. For example, we have a large School of Music with many different programs and majors. The Music subject area in the database needed to meet its diverse needs. To keep related choices together, we used subheadings such as "Music-Vocal/Choral" and "Music-Jazz."

Allowing flexibility in Source Types was necessary. The mean number of Source Types used per subject is eight, but some subjects have as many as fourteen. We currently have seventy-two Source Types defined in the database. Some are used only for one subject area, such as "Percussion" within "Music-Instrumental," "Industry Classifications" within "Business" and "Iconography" within "Art."

Two alphabetical sets of rankings were not enough for some of our librarians, who wanted more control in how the items displayed. A modification to the initial database allowed librarians to sequentially rank as many items as they desired. Thus, the librarian could determine the order of all the items on the list by ranking them 1, 2, 3, etc. Alternatively, the librarian could rank several of the items and leave the others unranked, meaning they would display alphabetically. Although this feature is useful during the initial creation of a subject category, it is more problematic when records are being added or deleted later. The person making the changes must check to see what type of ranking was used and take care not to inadvertently change the ranking structure.

One of the more lighthearted aspects of the project was deciding on a name. Everyone working on the project was invited to submit possible names. Many of the choices emphasized the purpose of the database–to find information by subject. "Guide Guru," "Subject Deity," "The Path," and "Info Gateway" fell into this category. Several, like "Dynamic Data" and "PopUp Guide" focused on the interactive nature of the database. Others tried to integrate the university's mascot, a pirate. Choices within this genre included "Pirate Loot," "Pirate Treasure," "Pirate Picks," and the eventual winner, "Pirate Source." We planned to use the name in marketing to create brand identity and instant recognition of the database, particularly among our primary audience of undergraduate students. We obtained permission from the university's licensing office to use the ECU Pirate logo on our pages.

We began entering data for Pirate Source in February 2001, using a data entry form created in Microsoft Access. Data input continued in earnest throughout the spring, summer and fall. At least fifteen people in the department, including several graduate students, contributed to the database. Two reference librarians served as editors, proofing content and checking for uniformity. Sources we used for selecting and describing resources included:

- our existing subject guides and bibliographies
- Librarian's Index to the Internet
- The Scout Report
- Infomine
- The ResourceShelf
- Lawrence Looks at Books
- Reference Books Bulletin
- Choice
- American Reference Books Annual

- Guide to Reference Books (Robert Balay, editor)
- Walford's Guide to Reference Materials
- Subject Encyclopedias: User Guide, Review Citations, and Keyword Index
- publishers' Web sites
- recommendations from faculty in academic departments on campus
- monographic guides to bibliographic research for particular subject areas (Libraries Unlimited and G.K. Hall were two favorite publishers)
- our reference department "new acquisitions" shelf

Later, our systems department created a Web-based data input form using PHP. This form gave us more flexibility as to the number of people who could enter data and the locations from which they could work. For security reasons, we limited access to the input forms by IP address. The data input form uses a combination of free text and controlled vocabulary. Controlled vocabulary terms, presented in the form of drop-down menus, are used for subject, source type, format, access restrictions, and limit (resource must be used in the library, Web-based, or none). We use a proxy server to provide access to subscription databases from off-campus. If specific access restrictions are selected on the input form, a script automatically adds a base URL to the associated Web address so that the users attempting to access the resource from off-campus must be verified through the proxy server. Free text is used for title, description, rank and location (call number or URL).

The input form includes a search feature. Our procedures call for librarians to use the search feature before a title is added. If a record already exists for the title, the librarian should add the desired subject to the existing record. The librarian will be able to edit the description, set the ranking order and source type associated with the display for the new subject, and add a format. If the librarian tries to add a duplicate title, an error message will be generated, but not until the end of the process when the completed record is submitted for addition to the database.

To simplify the public display, we decided to use graphics to convey some of the information included in the record. Icons indicate if access is restricted to the university community, if an item is freely available on the Web, or if the item must be used in the library. These icons include alternate text useful to persons using text-only browsers or readers, as well as a link to additional information about the meaning of each specific access restriction. Similarly, a small image of a page indicates that a Web-based resource contains a significant amount of fulltext material. In this way, the results list conveys a great deal of information the student needs in a compact and attractive manner.

The Web-based front-end interface to the database was originally created using Cold Fusion and SQL. Because of library concerns about robustness and programming flexibility, MySQL, Java and PHP were used for the production database.

FIRST EXPERIENCES WITH THE LIVE DATABASE

Pirate Source went live in December 2001, with fifty-five subjects and approximately 1,300 records. We promoted Pirate Source in the student and faculty newspapers as "your source for the best resources on a topic." Quotes from students who used Pirate Source for the first time were included in one of the articles. One student noted that "You've got all your subjects right here on one screen and you don't have to go looking around on all the other sites [. . .]. Pretty much every subject you could study, you can find everything on it right here." A computer science professor declared "I LOVE this site! Many thanks. I am making my first assignment in my class to use this site."

Experience with Pirate Source led to several improvements to the database. We added a Source Type for "subject specialist," thus incorporating our strongest resource of all, our knowledgeable librarians, into the database. We saw that the most common error was caused by the failure of users to select the desired Source Type, so we made "All Sources" the default selection. The user can override this selection by clicking in one or more boxes to select the desired source types. We also rearranged the order in which Source Types displayed; instead of an alphabetical display, we can "push" the "Starting Points" Source Type to the top of the list, or customize the display in other ways. And, of course, we continued to add subjects to Pirate Source. As of April 2003, Pirate Source contained 2,150 records, covering seventy-one subject areas.

USE BY STUDENTS

The difficulties of navigating a large academic library can be intimidating and confusing for many students. Undergraduate students tend to take courses in many different subject areas so that even if they are comfortable doing research in their major area, other topics might leave them stumped. Even more savvy researchers can have trouble locating appropriate journal articles or identifying useful reference tools. Graduate students are perceived as more advanced researchers but many of them are returning students who may feel intimidated by changes that have occurred in libraries since their college days. Graduate students who are more familiar with library research will be expected to work on a higher level and may not know of all the resources available to them. Pirate Source is designed to give students at any level carefully selected starting points from which they can begin their research.

For the student working in an unfamiliar subject area, Pirate Source provides a single access point for print reference sources, print, CD ROM, and online indexes, full-text databases, government documents, and free Web sites. If students can remember just two access points, Pirate Source and the catalog, they are well equipped to conduct the research needed for the majority of their assignments. Pirate Source results can be customized to display the particular type of sources the user is seeking. The user first chooses a subject area (see Figure 1). In the next step, the user can limit the results according to the source type(s) needed (see Figure 2). Finally, the user is presented with a customized list of sources (see Figure 3).

For the user completely unfamiliar with the subject area being researched, Pirate Source will provide a list of encyclopedias, dictionaries, handbooks, etc., appropriate for the subject. The user could then get the important background information, basic facts including dates and spellings, before attempting searches of databases or the catalog.

Choosing the best article databases for a specific topic can be a daunting task. Even smaller libraries now have access to a large number of databases through consortia or statewide licensing programs. Joyner Library offers access to over 150 databases. There are several problems for the user in selecting useful databases. The first is the difference between databases that offer only indexing and abstracting, those that have a large percentage of fulltext coverage, and those that contain only fulltext coverage. The names of databases often reflect company affiliation rather than content. There is no intuitive link between ERIC and education or between LexisNexis Academic and news or legal research. Pirate Source addresses these difficulties by listing databases by subject area (general databases such as InfoTrac Expanded Academic ASAP show up under many of the subjects) and by including an icon that indicates which ones contain a large proportion of fulltext coverage.

FIGURE 1

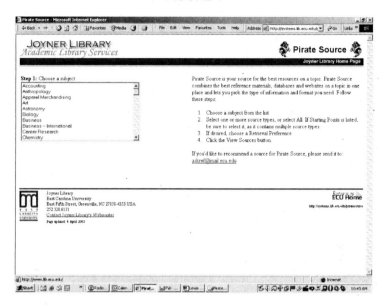

FIGURE 2

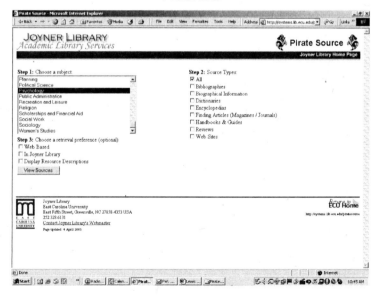

FIGURE 3

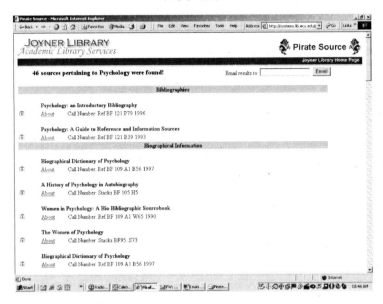

Students sometimes have trouble understanding the differences between information formats. A serious problem that many of us encounter at the reference desk is the confusion over the scope and nature of what is available free online. Many of us have heard students say something to the effect that "I have already searched the Internet and couldn't find information on my topic." Students are often confused about the differences between the free Web and subscription databases. Exclusive dependence on online sources can keep students from using print sources–even if they are the most appropriate for their project. Pirate Source is designed to help overcome these problems and guide students toward the best sources for their topics.

In the Pirate Source display, format is instantly apparent. Print sources and CD ROMs have call numbers. The titles of online sources–subscription or free–are active links. Icons to the left of the titles indicate if the source is a free Web site, a subscription database that we have access to through NC LIVE (North Carolina libraries' statewide database acquisition and licensing program), or a database we are subscribing to independently. Users can click on a link labeled "about" to get a short description of the item. Integrating the sources and displaying them together in this way has two important advantages for the student user. The first is that it encourages users to select sources according to the information they contain rather than format. Fewer users will search article databases for facts best found in reference sources. The second is that the distinction is made between free online sources and subscription databases. Hopefully, this will help to reinforce this important distinction in the minds of our users.

LIBRARY FACULTY AND STAFF USE

Pirate Source is also a useful tool for library faculty and staff. Library personnel use Pirate Source for e-mail questions, at the reference desk, in research consultations, and in bibliographic instruction. Pages in Pirate Source can also be created for specific research topics that do not fit well into the academic subject classification.

Answering e-mail questions can be a challenge because one starts with only the information the user has given. No reference interview takes place. It is possible to misunderstand the question and therefore mislead the user. Many of the questions we receive through our e-mail reference service are about how to find information rather than a query for a specific fact. Users usually write that they are doing a paper on X or looking for information about Y. Our responses, therefore, tend to refer them to a source or list of sources such as the catalog, a reference tool, or an article database. Referring the patron to Pirate Source can give them a good start. They get an extensive list of sources in a variety of formats. Users who cannot come to the library can choose to view only online sources. They also get short explanations of what the sources contain so that they can evaluate them before doing a search.

For traditional in-person questions at the reference desk, Pirate Source is heavily used. Students are not the only ones who do not always know where to look when confronted with an unfamiliar research topic. Anyone who has worked a public service desk in a library has had this experience. Reference faculty and staff use Pirate Source to overcome this difficulty. This process of discovery for us is an excellent opportunity for instructing the user on library use. Showing the user how to use Pirate Source, explaining the different kinds of sources included in it and how to access them, and talking about the research discovery process from a cold start makes the collection more transparent and helps the user to be more independent. The same process occurs in scheduled individual research consultations. After demonstrating Pirate Source and discussing ways to get started in research, the Pirate Source results can be printed for the user to take home or to the stacks.

Pirate Source is also used extensively in bibliographic instruction. At East Carolina University, bibliographic instruction is conducted in fifty or seventy-five minute one-shot class meetings. The students in a typical class arrive with greatly varying levels of information literacy. In most classes–especially those for first and second semester composition courses–we have to assume that our students are entirely innocent of library skills and focus on the basics. Because of the amount of time it takes to explain the purpose and use of the catalog, how to locate books within the library, general library services like interlibrary loan, and how to find journal articles, it is difficult to include an explanation of how to evaluate sources and choose those most appropriate for academic research. We have found that in demonstrations, Pirate Source is useful both as a subject guide and as a graphic representation of the variety of formats in which one finds high-quality information.

A demonstration of Pirate Source is a good opportunity to pass on a few tips about the general organization of information. The initial choice of a subject area gives the students a chance to reflect on who in the academy might be studying their topic and in what types of sources the information might be published. For some common assignments that do not fit easily into an academic subject area such as career research, grants, and scholarships and financial aid, topic-specific pages have been created. For most topics, however, the user must decide which subject area(s) to check. In classes, this step is an opportunity for the instructor to give a few remarks about the origination of information and how a paper topic might overlap several academic disciplines.

The displays of materials in Pirate Source usually contain a variety of formats. Most common are print reference sources, online subscription databases, and free Web sites. Since many users have a bias toward online sources and do not understand the differences between a free site and a subscription database, this is an excellent opportunity to give them an explanation. In bibliographic instruction, we can explain that information is a valuable commodity and "you get what you pay for." The discussion of the source display is a good time to talk about bias in information and discuss the possible motivations for giving information away for free. A demonstration of Pirate Source in bibliographic instruction allows librarians to offer students a good starting point for research and an opportunity to discuss the variety of available information formats and their relative merits.

Pirate Source was developed as a response to a perceived user need. The proliferation of information formats spurred by advances in technology left our users confused and ill-informed about where to look for appropriate information sources for their research projects. Many users labor under the false impression that everything they need is available on the free portion of the Web. It can be a daunting task for the uninitiated to locate even basic reference sources on their topic in a large academic library. Because so many users do not know where to look for information or how to recognize information appropriate for academic projects when they encounter it, a tool was needed to aid them. Traditional subject guides seemed inadequate to meet the challenges of these problems.

A dynamic database such as Pirate Source has many advantages over traditional, static subject guides. It can be updated and modified by many contributors without the need for knowledge of HTML or any scripting language. Updates can be made on the fly and across the database so that a title can be added or removed from multiple subject areas at the same time. The impact of staff changes is minimized because new people can be trained quickly to take over responsibility for a subject area and to make additions and changes to the database. It is easy to use and updates take effect quickly. This type of database is also extremely flexible. New subject areas can be created at any time to respond to user needs and the subject guides can be arranged in the fashion that best suits the mission of the library. It is easy for patrons to use. They can find call numbers for reference sources quickly or link to databases or free Web sites directly from the results list. It is very useful to librarians and staff at the reference desk and is a useful didactic tool in bibliographic instruction.

Our satisfaction with Pirate Source has been high and we get positive feedback about it from faculty and students. However, nothing is perfect and there are a few additions we would like to see in the future. The first would be the ability to generate statistics about use. We would also like to be able to delete records without the administrator's intervention. Finally, it would be useful if we could e-mail the source lists with active links. This would be especially helpful in answering e-mail questions. The project has been a success and has increased library transparency and usability for our users, and addressed the need for a single starting point that includes sources in all formats.

SELECTED LIST OF SOURCES

Antelman, Kristin. "Getting Out of the HTML Business: The Database-Driven Web Site Solution." *Information Technology and Libraries* 18 (1999): 176-181.

Cullen, Kevin F. "PHP: An Open Source Solution for Web Programming and Dynamic Content." *Information Technology and Libraries* 21 (2002): 116-120.

Fagan, Jody C. "Transition to a Unified System: Using Perl to Drive Library Databases and Enhance Web Site Functionality." *The Electronic Library* 19 (2001): 168-179.

Galván-Estrada, Laura. "Moving Towards a User-Centered Database-Driven Web Site at the UCSD Libraries." *Internet Reference Services Quarterly* 7 (2002): 49-61.

Hein, Karen K., and Marc W. Davis. "The Research Wizard: An Innovative Web Application for Patron Service." *Internet Reference Services Quarterly* 7 (2002): 1- 18.

Jaffe, Lee. "Exploring Dynamic Web Sites with Databases: The UC Santa Cruz Experience." *Library Computing* 19 (2000): 35-41.

Platt, Mary. "Databases to the Web: From Static to Dynamic on the Express." *Internet Reference Services Quarterly* 7 (2002): 113-121.

Westman, Stephen. "Building Database-Backed Web Applications: Process and Issues." *Information Technology and Libraries* 21 (2002): 63-72.

Westman, Stephen. "Database-Backed Library Web Pages." *The Electronic Library* 19 (2001): 424-431.

Westra, Brian. "HealthLinks: A ColdFusion Web Application." *Internet Reference Services Quarterly* 7 (2002): 63-88.

REFERENCE

Roberts, Gary. "Designing a Database-Drive Web Site, or, the Evolution of the Info-Iguana." *Computers in Libraries* (Oct. 2000): 26+, ProQuest Research Library, ProQuest. Joyner Library. 29 March 2003. <http://proquest.umi.com/>.

Electronic Journals
in Aggregated Collections:
Providing Access Through the Catalog
and a Cold Fusion Database

Sue Anderson

SUMMARY. Patrons in academic libraries want convenient 24-hour access to full-text journals in a rapid, convenient manner. They want "anytime, anywhere" access to information and they do not want to enter a library to obtain it. This article describes how Eastern Washington University Libraries provide access to full-text journals through several collections. *[Article copies available for a fee from The Haworth Document Delivery Service: 1-800-HAWORTH. E-mail address: <docdelivery@haworthpress.com> Website: <http://www.HaworthPress.com> © 2005 by The Haworth Press, Inc. All rights reserved.]*

KEYWORDS. Electronic publishing, full-text journals, full-text aggregators, OCLC ECO, URL, aggregators

Sue Anderson is Acquisitions and Electronic Resources Librarian, Eastern Washington University Libraries, 100 LIB, 816 F Street, Cheney, WA 99004 (E-mail: sanderson@mail.ewu.edu).

[Haworth co-indexing entry note]: "Electronic Journals in Aggregated Collections: Providing Access Through the Catalog and a Cold Fusion Database." Anderson, Sue. Co-published simultaneously in *The Acquisitions Librarian* (The Haworth Information Press, an imprint of The Haworth Press, Inc.) No. 33/34, 2005, pp. 121-131; and: *Managing Digital Resources in Libraries* (ed: Audrey Fenner) The Haworth Information Press, an imprint of The Haworth Press, Inc., 2005, pp. 121-131. Single or multiple copies of this article are available for a fee from The Haworth Document Delivery Service [1-800-HAWORTH, 9:00 a.m. - 5:00 p.m. (EST). E-mail address: docdelivery@haworthpress.com].

INTRODUCTION

Students attending classes at Eastern Washington University want information now! They want access to full-text journals via a computer–not only from the library, but from their dorm rooms, homes, or even from distance education sites. Faculty members also want the same kind of access to these journals from their offices. Students and faculty do not, and, in some cases cannot, come to the library to look for periodical articles. From the many publishers, societies, and aggregators who offer access to full-text articles, we chose several vendors to provide access to these articles for our patrons.

This article addresses how Eastern Washington University Libraries selected full-text aggregators and collections, implemented titles into the OPAC and Cold Fusion database, and encountered and overcame problems in providing access to these full-text journals.

BACKGROUND

Eastern Washington University (EWU) is located in Cheney, in the eastern part of Washington State. EWU is a regional, comprehensive university offering undergraduate and masters degree programs. EWU has about 9,100 students; 7,000 at its Cheney campus and 2,100 at its shared campus with Washington State University (WSU) in Spokane. The Spokane campus shares a combined library with WSU and both institutions conduct classes in the same buildings. Students may attend classes at both institutions at this combined campus. The main WSU campus is located in Pullman, about 100 miles south of Spokane, with additional branch campuses in Vancouver and Richland.

EWU and WSU libraries share an integrated library system by Innovative Interfaces, Inc (III). The libraries maintain a union catalog called Griffin in which they share bibliographic records, but each has individual item and order records in the combined OPAC. Students can search for all items owned by participating libraries or branches, or limit to an individual library. EWU and WSU participate in a state consortium to purchase access to various full-text databases and aggregators. Every library in both systems maintains its own home page distinctive to its campus. Each institution also provides access to full-text databases and aggregators in its own way.

READY FOR CHANGE

In the past, patrons had to come to the library to locate information. Librarians purchased paper periodicals and stored them in the building. Patrons used print periodical indexes to locate articles, find journals in the stacks and then locate printed articles in the issue. Even in the first manifestation of the OPAC, patrons could locate journal titles in the on-line catalog.

But students have changed, and their idea of what the library should provide and how it should be provided has also changed. Students are busy and want "convenient, 24-hour access to journals" (Hughes, 148) from their homes and dorm rooms. Distance education students need access to our material with a convenient and rapid mode of delivery. In the past, we provided students with material through interlibrary loan, which often took days or weeks to arrive. For these reasons, we decided to provide access to full-text general interest and business periodicals through aggregators.

SELECTION OF A FULL-TEXT AGGREGATOR

In 1999, the Washington State Legislature provided funds to the six baccalaureate institutions in the state to select an electronic full-text journal package. In addition to EWU, these institutions included the University of Washington, Washington State University, Western Washington University, Central Washington University and The Evergreen State College. The group, called the Washington Cooperative Library Project (WCLP), selected one librarian to manage the project. He invited several companies that provided full-text journal packages to submit proposals to WCLP. The WCLP looked at a general interest core of materials that would benefit undergraduate students, and also examined business and scientific journal packages for upper level and graduate students. The group selected criteria, drew up questions and asked librarians at each institution to look through trial databases of several vendors. Once the trial was finished, WCLP selected several ProQuest databases for a three-year contract.

In 2002, the ProQuest contract was available for renewal. Although ProQuest had provided a good product for patrons, WCLP asked for bids from a number of full-text aggregators for the next three-year term. WCLP went through the same procedure. Librarians at the six institutions used trial databases for several weeks, helping students at reference desks as well as testing all databases with various queries. WCLP selected ProQuest for another three-year contract.

IMPLEMENTING ACCESS TO FULL-TEXT JOURNALS

In 1999, when the Washington Cooperative Library Project selected the first ProQuest database package, each institution decided how to provide access to full-text titles in the ProQuest databases on its campus. EWU chose to provide access in two ways.

Access Through the OPAC

Eastern Washington University Library imports MARC records from OCLC for print titles. Students and faculty were accustomed to searching the OPAC for a title and locating issues on the shelves. When librarians discussed how to provide access to full-text titles, we made a decision to use the single bibliographic record approach and attach a URL link to the full-text database in a print record. Reference librarians stated that students, especially those in distance education courses, would benefit from this single record approach because they would find a title that contained print and electronic access with one result. EWU librarians also believe that our OPAC should reflect a complete index of what we own as well as what we license and "the catalog allows the library to display availability of (and provide access to) electronic resources in the context of the library's entire collection" (Nilges, 315).

EWU started adding links to the OPAC by printing title lists from ProQuest, beginning with Medical Library and Business Periodicals online. We added a URL link to the 856 field in the MARC record of every print title in the OPAC that was also available full-text in ProQuest. The URL linked to the search page in ProQuest; the patron had to retype the journal title or keywords to locate the article. This solution was not ideal for our patrons because it does not link directly to the journal title, issue or article, but the patron had access to the full-text article, which was the goal.

Adding the same link to ProQuest for a large number of titles is tedious, so we set up macros within the staff module of our integrated library system (ILS) to add links from our system to ProQuest. We also provide remote access to our full-text journals through our Web site for students outside the library. While the systems librarian created the remote link, we created another macro in our ILS to add the off-campus remote link to ProQuest.

EWU does not have a print subscription for every full-text title available on the ProQuest databases. For Medical Library and Business Periodicals Online titles for which we do not have a print subscription, we import a bibliographic record from OCLC and add on-campus and off-campus URL links from each MARC record to ProQuest's search page.

Access Through the Cold Fusion Database

EWU also provides a second way to access full-text articles using a Cold Fusion database. At the time of the initial three-year contract with ProQuest, one of our librarians created the Cold Fusion database with a member of the campus computer department. Using the first two title lists from ProQuest, the librarian added titles and URLs to Cold Fusion. On the Cold Fusion search page, patrons type a journal title or keywords, or click on a letter of the alphabet to locate a journal title. Once they click on the title, the link takes them directly to the aggregator or collection search screen.

Staff members, who added URL links in the staff module of III, also added the on-campus and off-campus URL links in the Cold Fusion database. This process was very time-consuming and tedious and then slowed to a crawl if not a complete stop when the librarian and computer staff person resigned from their positions at EWU. One staff member in our department continued to add URL links to the titles in the Cold Fusion database and waited for a replacement to be hired to continue the project.

A new librarian was hired and slowly restarted the project. For a short time, we had a problem adding new titles to Cold Fusion. Once that problem was fixed, we started to add new titles and URL links to the Cold Fusion database.

ADDING ANOTHER COLLECTION

After implementation of our first aggregation of full-text journals, students and faculty used full-text online journals to a greater extent than print journals. Librarians conducted instruction classes on how to access and search databases, print and e-mail articles. They answered telephone inquiries on the same topics from distance education students.

EWU decided to add access to other full-text journals through OCLC and its Electronic Collections Online (ECO) database. We started by adding full-text journals for some of our print subscription titles. The Collection Development Coordinator selected the first titles, and sent the list to staff members who added URL links to the MARC record of each print title. During the following few years, the Collection Development Coordinator continued to select new titles, renew or cancel titles and track all aspects of this ECO collection.

When EWU hired the Acquisitions and Electronic Resources Librarian in July of 2001, the Collection Development Coordinator turned over the ECO collection to her. Within the year, EWU librarians created an ECO policy covering title selection, renewal and cancellation. We also established criteria for selection based on whether we had a print subscription, if that title was on the Print Subscriber Program list, and whether library or departmental funds had been used to purchase the print subscription. The Print Subscriber Program consists of a group of publishers who make electronic versions of over 1,600 journals available, at no additional subscription cost through Electronic Collections Online, to institutions that subscribe to the print version of those titles. EWU set a limit on the additional cost we will pay for a title we have in print that is not on the Print Subscriber Program but paid for with library or departmental funds.

In the fall of 2002, the ECO policy eased the renewal process. Parameters of the policy determined which titles to add, renew, or cancel. Because we only add current print titles to our ECO list, we canceled titles we had not renewed in the summer. Currently, we still have access to back files of titles we canceled. When we considered whether to retain current titles or add new ones, we looked at the 2003 vendors on the Print Subscriber Program. Because cost is always a factor, we looked first at those titles. We also looked at which funds we used to purchase print titles. We have more leeway in purchasing online access if print titles were purchased with library funds rather than departmental funds.

During the past year, we started to add ending dates to our URL links in the OPAC and Cold Fusion database, a process which requires more work for our staff. However, when patrons locate a title in either database, they see coverage dates for titles and can determine whether a particular article is available.

DIFFERENCES IN COLLECTIONS

ProQuest and Electronic Collections Online databases are useful in different ways. We purchased access to a group of ProQuest titles for a three-year period and paid a specific price for a range of titles that will change throughout the contract period. This macro title selection covered a wide range of titles with one purchase. Every two weeks we receive e-mail updates from ProQuest on title changes, cessations and cancellations. Titles are added, dropped, or closed. Embargo periods, ranging from 30 to 730 days, are added or dropped. Full-text, text and graphics or image are added or discontinued. We receive this information before changes are made on the ProQuest database. We wait two to three weeks, check titles on the ProQuest database, then make changes in the OPAC and Cold Fusion. These e-mail updates concerning coverage changes would be more valuable if changes coincided with e-mail notification.

At the end of the year, we select, renew or cancel individual titles from ECO and have access for the following year. Once a month OCLC notifies libraries about new titles added to the Electronic Collections Online. We check that list against our print collection and add any title for which we have a current subscription. At the time of renewal, we pay a fee for the selected titles for the entire year. If we add additional titles during the year, we pay for those titles as we add them. Our cost for ECO access changes from year to year based on the number of titles we select.

AGGREGATOR AND COLLECTION PROBLEMS

Lack of continuous access to titles is one problem with aggregated collections. "Unfortunately, since aggregators do not own the full-text content they offer on their platforms, they are dependent on the publishers who own the content" (Brunelle, 298). In our ProQuest collection, titles are canceled, discontinued or added throughout the year. We have access to content at the beginning of a contract that we may not have at the end. In our ECO collection, we have access throughout the year. When we renew each year, ECO has a list of titles from various vendors from which we choose. We also can choose titles from publishers who charge an added fee for online access to their journals. Aggregators receive access to titles from publishers with no surety for perpetual access to those titles. Libraries understand that they purchase access to online titles, not the titles themselves. However, we want perpetual archival access to online journals just as we have with printed periodicals which we retain on shelves for as long as we wish.

UPDATING HOLDINGS IN THE DATABASES

When ProQuest removes titles from their database, we remove the URL link in three places if we have a print subscription: from the on-campus and off-campus links in the MARC record in the OPAC and from the Cold Fusion database. If we do not have a print subscription to a title, we delete the bibliographic and item records from the OPAC. In Cold Fusion, we simply delete the entire record. Though very time-intensive, we remove titles from the OPAC and Cold Fusion databases to keep them accurate.

If we cancel access to a title in ECO, we continue to have archival access to any back files of that title if we had a print subscription. For that reason, we add ending dates to our holdings in the OPAC and Cold Fusion.

COLD FUSION PROBLEMS

Cold Fusion has its drawbacks. EWU libraries lack complete control of the database, and must rely on another department within the institution when problems arise. Barring that, the database works well. Adding and editing titles is easy, albeit time-consuming. It is also easy to add new titles because we have the ability to copy and paste URL links from the OPAC to Cold Fusion.

On EWU library's home page, patrons choose a link to library databases. Under databases, they choose the OPAC or Cold Fusion. Since the OPAC is a complete index of what we own onsite and what we have licensed, the Cold Fusion offers another way for patrons to look at full-text journals. EWU staff is constantly updating electronic journal information in our collections.

TRACKING USAGE STATISTICS

"Statistics of how many times a resource is accessed are important to determine if that resource is really needed, or if it is worth the price paid" (VanGoethem, 172). Currently, we look at usage statistics in ECO. We look at database usage, time of day searches are made, number of searches and downloads, and whether searches are made from within the library or from off-campus. We can use this information to determine if we chose appropriate titles for patron use, or if we should retain or cancel a particular title.

Accessing a title without an accompanying download of an article may not necessarily be a reason to cancel a title. We have all looked at a title in an issue of a journal, read the abstract and glanced through the article without copying it. Merely looking at number of searches does not necessarily mean much. Downloading or e-mailing articles is a better indication of a journal's use for patrons.

FUTURE

EWU will continue using the OPAC and Cold Fusion as two ways to offer access to full-text journals. Librarians view the OPAC as our complete index of everything we have onsite as well as what we access and license. We also have the Cold Fusion database to provide another access point for our electronic journals in a secondary database. It is a product that responds to our needs and serves our patrons. We can customize Cold Fusion by adding paid or free single titles, government document journals, and other resources.

We anticipate budget cuts this year and next. Our state legislature anticipates the budget climate will not change much in the next five years. With this gloomy forecast and possibly more budget constraints in the future, we hope to keep our current staffing as it exists. We have talked with representatives of Serials Solution and TDNet and looked at their journal management products. Both appear to be an easier method for managing journals than the one we are currently using. In the future, we might find or reallocate funds to make the change or determine that it is worth our staff time to do so.

CONCLUSION

Electronic journal collections present management challenges to libraries. Aggregators provide a collection of full-text electronic journals, either in a general interest collection or in subject interest groups.

Purchasing access to an aggregated collection is a "one-stop shopping solution" for many libraries like EWU because the selection is macro, rather than micro. It is easier to purchase access to a collection as a group rather than singly title by title. However, when we purchase access to a group of titles, some may not be useful to any of our patrons. This is not any different from purchasing print titles. Libraries have titles on their shelves that are seldom or never used.

Perpetual, archival access to titles is another problem of full-text titles in aggregated collections. Titles come and go within these collections and libraries have no control over what the collection maintains. Librarians add and delete titles and close access in OPACs and journal management databases as they manage electronic full-text titles. Managing electronic journals is a continual, ongoing process. At least for now, with ECO titles, as we select and deselect, we retain access to back issues for titles we have purchased in print.

The dual way in which EWU manages electronic journal access in aggregators and collections is somewhat cumbersome. We spend time and energy adding and deleting URL links in our OPAC and Cold Fusion database. This work is time- and staff-intensive. We could save time and energy using a journal management product and simplify our process. However, budget constraints and choices preclude that option at this time. Since we created the Cold Fusion database, we decide what to add, whether several titles from publishers, single titles or government documents. Using this database gives us some freedom.

"Electronic journals offer librarians a renewed hope that we can continue to provide responsive service and to provide access to information" (McMillan, 128). Every library chooses the best way to provide access to electronic journals in aggregators and collections based on service to its clientele, budget constraints, staff time and expertise. EWU librarians are trying to provide the best service for our patrons by adding full-text titles in our OPAC and Cold Fusion database. Adding electronic journals to the OPAC is a way to include access to these journals that exist outside of the collection of items we own and house in our libraries. EWU created the Cold Fusion database in response to our patrons' needs. The database serves as a secondary avenue for electronic journal access for our patrons. EWU will continue to use aggregators and collections to supply full-text journals for our patrons. Full-text titles will remain a core component in our library for student and faculty use.

REFERENCES

Brunelle, Bette. "Quieting the Crowd: The Clamour for Full-text." *Online & CD-ROM Review* 23 (1999): 297-302.

Hughes, Janet A., and Catherine A. Lee. "Giving Patrons What They Want: The Promise, Process and Pitfalls of Providing Full-text Access to Journals." *Collection Building* 17 (1998): 148-153.

McMillan, Gail. "Electronic Journals: Access through Libraries." *The Virtual Library: Visions and Realities.* Ed. Laverna M. Saunders. Westport, CT: Meckler Publishing, 1993. 111-129.

Nilges, Chris. "Evolving an Integrated Electronic Journals Solution: OCLC FirstSearch Electronic Collections Online." *The Serials Librarian* 33 (1998): 299-318.

Van Goethem, Jeri. "Buying, Leasing and Connecting to Electronic Information: The Changing Scene of Library Acquisitions." *New Automation Technology for Acquisitions and Collection Development.* Ed. Rosann Bazirjian. New York: The Haworth Press, Inc., 1995. 165-174.

Just Another Format: Integrating Resources for Users of Personal Digital Assistants

Denise Koufogiannakis
Pam Ryan
Susan Dahl

SUMMARY. This article discusses the integration of library resources for users of personal digital assistants (PDAs), with a focus on collections issues within an academic environment. The University of Alberta Libraries' PDA services initiative is used as an example of integrating

Denise Koufogiannakis is Collections Manager, John W. Scott Health Sciences Library, University of Alberta, 2K3.17 Walter C. Mackenzie Health Sciences Centre, Edmonton, Alberta, T6G 2R7, Canada (E-mail: denise.koufogiannakis@ualberta. ca). Pam Ryan is Research and Special Projects Librarian, University of Alberta Libraries, 5-02 Cameron Library, Edmonton, Alberta, T6G 2J8, Canada (E-mail: pam.ryan@ualberta.ca). Susan Dahl is Metadata and Cataloguing Librarian, University of Alberta Libraries, 5-25C Cameron Library, Edmonton, Alberta, T6G 2J8, Canada (E-mail: susan.dahl@ualberta.ca).

[Haworth co-indexing entry note]: "Just Another Format: Integrating Resources for Users of Personal Digital Assistants." Koufogiannakis, Denise, Pam Ryan, and Susan Dahl. Co-published simultaneously in *The Acquisitions Librarian* (The Haworth Information Press, an imprint of The Haworth Press, Inc.) No. 33/34, 2005, pp. 133-145; and: *Managing Digital Resources in Libraries* (ed: Audrey Fenner) The Haworth Information Press, an imprint of The Haworth Press, Inc., 2005, pp. 133-145. Single or multiple copies of this article are available for a fee from The Haworth Document Delivery Service [1-800-HAWORTH, 9:00 a.m. - 5:00 p.m. (EST). E-mail address: docdelivery@haworthpress.com].

http://www.haworthpress.com/web/AL
Digital Object Identifier: 10.1300/J101v17n33_12

services and resources into a library collection. Licensing issues, loaning of PDA books on expansion cards, cataloguing and processing of PDA books, and making existing resources PDA-accessible are all discussed. Although PDA integration is still at the early stages within libraries, there is much that libraries can do to support users of personal digital assistants. *[Article copies available for a fee from The Haworth Document Delivery Service: 1-800-HAWORTH. E-mail address: <docdelivery@haworthpress.com> Website: <http://www.HaworthPress.com> © 2005 by The Haworth Press, Inc. All rights reserved.]*

KEYWORDS. Personal Digital Assistants, handheld devices, portable computers, academic libraries, college and university libraries, collection development, cataloging rules

INTRODUCTION

Resources for Personal Digital Assistants (PDAs) are one of the newest formats that librarians are beginning to integrate into library collections. How does a library integrate service and collection development models for PDA users into its existing services? What are the issues faced when attempting to license content that is PDA compatible? How are PDA-accessible resources selected, catalogued and stored when some are the size of a postage stamp? How do librarians integrate existing collections into a PDA-accessible user-service model? This paper presents the issues that need to be considered for the development of an integrated academic library collections program that supports users of Personal Digital Assistants.

PDAs AND ACADEMIC LIBRARIES: WHAT'S HAPPENING IN USER SERVICES?

Reports of PDA service initiatives in academic libraries have begun to appear in the published library literature in recent years, but certainly not to the same extent that the health sciences literature indicates health care professionals are using PDAs to access reference sources and other point-of-care information. Searches of *Library Literature* and *Library and Information Science Abstracts* (LISA) result in a number of technology trend articles that highlight possibilities for PDA services and application in libraries (Bridges; Galganski; John; Ross; Schuyler; Shipman; Smith; Stoddard). However, the volume of literature describing PDA service development and implementation does not accurately reflect the number of PDA service initiatives currently taking place in academic libraries. Internet searches reveal more robust PDA initiatives than are reflected in the published literature and are a much better indicator of how prevalent the integration of PDA resources and services is becoming. Two particularly useful current awareness resources on the topic are the Hardin Library for the Health Sciences, University of Iowa, list of *Other Library PDA sites* and the *PDA Projects in Libraries* section of the Web site maintained by Megan Fox, Web and Electronic Resources Librarian, Simmons College Libraries. Many of these PDA service programs have been initiated by health sciences/medical libraries but there are programs of note in other subject areas and as system-wide initiatives.

Current PDA initiatives in academic libraries not only encompass the range of traditional library services but also include services not usually assumed by academic libraries. For example, some libraries provide technical support, training or tutorials for PDA hardware and software (OSF Saint Francis; Norris *Workshop Descriptions*; UTHSCSA *Tutorials*; Duke) or sponsor vendor demonstrations of PDA hardware, software, and accessories (Norris *PDA Fair*). Common PDA services include help and resource guides of PDA resources available for free or for cost on the Internet (Health Sciences Pittsburgh; Health Sciences UNC-Chapel Hill; UTHSCSA *PDA Resources*), Web bibliographies on PDAs and their use in specific disciplines (Virginia Commonwealth *Bibliography*; Arizona; UTHSCSA *PDA Bibliography*), and hardware buyers guides (University of Virginia Health Sciences Library; University of Illinois; Harvey Cushing). Some projects integrate PDA hardware by providing in-library PDA-accessible output devices with infrared beaming capabilities or syncing capabilities (Heisey; Himmelfarb *Pocket PC*; Himmelfarb *Palm*), or loan PDAs with pre-installed software (Library of the Health Sciences Peoria). Providing information about the library or library services (library hours, LC call number guide, library newsletters, e-mail reference form) in a PDA-accessible format is also widespread (Lincoln Trail; University of Georgia; Virginia Commonwealth *VCU Libraries To Go*; Western Kentucky). Collections services such as providing licensed PDA content and loaning PDA-accessible collections are also starting to take shape as more vendors pilot PDA-accessible information resources (University of Alberta *PDA Library Resources*; University of Arkansas).

THE UNIVERSITY OF ALBERTA PDA PROJECT

The resources of the University of Alberta Libraries comprise one of the largest research collections in Canada. The University of Alberta Libraries began offering PDA services in the Fall of 2001. The service initiative was the result of a noted increase in the number of people in the Library with PDAs, particularly residents and medical students. These groups of library users need information quickly and at the point of care, leading to the perfect fit with a handheld device that is easily portable and provides immediate, mobile access to information.

Like a number of other medical and health sciences libraries, the John W. Scott Health Sciences Library began by developing a Web page to group PDA-accessible health sciences resources that were available on the Internet. The Web page has since expanded into a central access point for all PDA services provided by the University of Alberta Libraries and was renamed the PDAZone.

To increase awareness of the library's role in providing information services for PDA users, librarians began to teach sessions entitled "Making the Most of your PDA." Sessions were immediately successful with good attendance. These sessions were also an opportunity to get to know University PDA users and their information needs. Sessions begin by asking participants to introduce themselves, indicate their discipline and University user group (faculty, student, resident) and discuss their PDA experience. Sessions ended with the distribution of a feedback questionnaire asking participants to indicate how the Library could enhance their PDA use and what resources and services they would like the Library to provide. These assessment methods informed decision-making as the integration of PDA-accessible resources into the Library's collection began.

Along with instruction sessions, the University of Alberta Libraries added several subject-specific and general resource guides to the PDAZone Web site. A mailing list for handheld users was established to facilitate exchange of information amongst interested parties; the Library's newsletter was formatted to be PDA-accessible via a popular service known as AvantGo <http://www.avantgo.com>; and an infrared (IR) beaming station was established within the Library for those wishing to beam database or catalogue search results instantly to their PDA.

PDA-specific resources that the University of Alberta Libraries have added to its collection include site-licensed, campus-wide access to the reference text PEPID <http://www.pepid.com>, as well as the complete collection of PDA-compatible Landes Bioscience handbooks <http://www.landesbioscience.com/handbooks/>. E-books on PDA expansion cards were also added to the collection for borrowing. The exploration of content availability in PDA format has led the librarians involved to note issues and challenges unique to this type of format, which need to be considered when beginning the integration of PDA products in a library environment. Licensing and cataloguing are two of the major issues librarians will face when attempting to integrate resources in this format.

LICENSING PDA RESOURCES

Deciding to support PDA services means having to cope with collections management issues that have a budgetary impact. In many cases, the content will be the same or similar to what the library already has in print or online. The decision then becomes whether or not to fund this same content in PDA-accessible format also. The University of Alberta Libraries decided to find ways to offer as much content as possible to library users in PDA format. This decision was based upon the demand for such content, and the desire to best serve users regardless of the format of the material.

Currently, there are not many resources available to be licensed for library use, although licensed delivery is now the norm for online journals and databases. Publishers of PDA products generally follow the one-PDA-one-download model, which makes licensed delivery of content more difficult. The idea of libraries providing content to PDA users is a new one to publishers, so in many cases the delivery model has not been clearly thought through. By exploring available PDA products on the Web, and through contact with publishers and vendors, it became clear that the PDA book market has not yet fully been opened to the world of libraries.

The different electronic delivery models for PDA content can be grouped into categories (Table 1), each with their unique pros and cons. When investigating a resource, collections librarians can easily determine which of these categories the product falls into, and whether or not that particular model fits with the service model of the library.

TABLE 1. Electronic Delivery Models of PDA Products

Model	Description
Free with existing licensed product	PDA content is free with the subscription to an existing licensed product.
User add-on purchase	Library users may independently purchase a PDA add-on if the library has an existing subscription or site license to the online product.
Institutional site license	An institutional site license is available for the PDA product with a set yearly cost, allowing as many downloads as is required.
Set number of downloads	The library must purchase a set range of downloads, often as an institutional add-on to an existing online product.
Electronic loaning with due dates	The library subscribes to an e-book system that allows loaning of PDA-compatible titles that expire from the device after a set time period.

Free with Existing Licensed Product

PDA content is free with the subscription to an existing licensed product. This would be the preferred format for most librarians trying to serve their users and balance the collections budget, however this seems to be the least offered option by publishers. Usually, if a library subscribes to an online product and a new PDA version is released, the library or its users will pay extra to obtain that content. One example of a product that does make its content available in PDA format is eMedicine <http://www.emedicine.com> (known as iMedicine for institutional subscribers). With this product, PDA versions of the available monographs are part of the package that is offered. If you are a subscriber to iMedicine, you have access to this content without added cost.

User Add-On Purchase

Library users may independently purchase a PDA add-on if the library has an existing subscription or site license to the online product. For example, the product Harrison's on Hand (HOH) <http://harrisons. accessmedicine.com/> offers a deal to individual subscribers whereby if their institution has a site license to Harrison's online, individuals at that institution can subscribe to HOH at a discounted price. Some libraries choose to advertise this as a benefit to their users. However, many libraries may not feel comfortable with this new role as an advertiser of products that users will need to pay for.

Institutional Site License

An institutional site license is available for the PDA product with a set yearly cost, allowing as many downloads as required. This is not a very popular option with publishers at this time, although it is the norm for e-journals and databases. The difference with PDAs is that the user must download the product to their own device. Some publishers have put measures in place so that the content will expire at the end of the contract period. Another issue is requiring users to verify their affiliation with the University before being able to download. Walk-in users to the library would not be able to download the product as they might an e-journal article, since the scope of the content is much more extensive. Products that currently follow this type of licensing model, which may have price differentials depending upon the size of the institution, are PEPID, InfoRetriever <http://www.infopoems.com/>, and Landes Bioscience.

Set Number of Downloads

The library must purchase a set range of downloads, often as an institutional add-on to an existing online product. This model is not based upon the size of an institution, but is instead purely based upon usage (or estimated usage) of the product. One obvious problem with this model is that if all paid downloads are used, payment for additional downloads will be required to ensure continued access to new users. This model may work well for libraries with flexible budgets. It can also be a good way to try out a product. However, as interest or PDA usage grows, costs could skyrocket. Two examples of this type of pricing model are the products OVID@hand <http://www.ovid.com> and PDXMD <http://www.pdxmd.com> which group numbers of users by 1-100, 101-250, etc., or charge a set rate per PDA download.

Electronic Loaning with Due Dates

The library subscribes to an e-book system that allows loaning of PDA-compatible titles that expire after a set time period. These types of systems, such as libwise <http://libwise.com> and OverDrive <http://www.overdrive.com/>, have just recently begun to take-off as an option for libraries. Cleveland Public Library <http://www.cpl.org> is one institution that has been an early adapter of this model. This type of e-book system presents a model based on the age-old premise of loaning individual books. An e-book is borrowed by a user, downloaded to the device of their choice (PDA, PC, laptop), and then expires from the device following the set borrowing period. The negative side of this model is that only one person can borrow a book at a time (unless multiple e-copies are purchased), and the time limit is restrictive in many disciplines such as medicine, where health care professionals need access to reference texts on their PDA continuously, without having to worry about access suddenly being erased.

LOANING BOOKS THE SIZE OF POSTAGE STAMPS

Since most PDAs come with expansion slots for memory cards (small cards the size of a postage stamp), another consideration for libraries is the purchase of e-books on expansion cards for loaning. This type of purchase allows libraries to integrate PDA books with other monographic material that may be available in various formats. Acquiring this type of book presents challenges simply due to the lack of available materials in this format. After an extensive search, the University of Alberta was able to purchase only a dozen or so academic titles on expansion cards for loaning purposes (University of Alberta *PDA Books*), the majority from Franklin Electronic Publishers <http://www.franklin. com/ebooks/>. Most publishers or vendors offer PDA products on a CD-ROM, allowing only one download per disc (considering copyright laws), or via an online download. The CD-ROM format is obviously not going to work in the traditional sense of loaning a book to a patron. However, the books on expansion cards do offer a potential solution, since the book is on a card that goes directly into the device, and only works when it is inserted. The cards are also secure, so that the book's content cannot be copied directly onto a PDA.

One issue that must be considered is the type of expansion card the book comes on (Table 2). Currently, there are different types of cards that are compatible with Palm OS, PocketPC OS, or even within the same operating system itself. Sony has their own type of card that generally does not work in other models, as do the older Handspring devices. Since there is no standard card, librarians are faced with the challenge of which format of e-book to buy: support one model, or buy multiple copies, supporting various devices. It is crucial to know library users' needs, including what format of device the majority are using.

TABLE 2. Types of PDA Expansion Cards for Books

Card Type	Compatible Devices
MultiMediaCard	Palm
Memory Stick	Sony, some PocketPCs
CompactFlash Card	PocketPC
SD (Secure Digital) Memory Card	Palm, some PocketPCs
Springboard Module	Handspring

Gathering feedback, via questionnaires, focus groups, or other means, is essential to making confident decisions.

CATALOGING AND PROCESSING PDA RESOURCES

Resources that are available in multiple formats, such as a PDA book on expansion card already held by a library in paper copy, present several issues for cataloguing. Formats can either be integrated on a single bibliographic record, or separate records can be created for each format to bring out their different features more effectively. The University of Alberta Libraries generally takes a single record approach to integrate print and online resources: the print record is supplemented with information about the online version. This approach proves to be more complex when integrating print and PDA resources, however. In this case, a multiple record approach has been adopted instead, because more information is required to describe the features of PDA cards adequately.

A note detailing system requirements for access to the e-book card is essential, so that users know if the card is compatible with their device's model. Moreover, if the library purchases multiple card formats for the same resource in order to accommodate different models, a separate record is created for each type of card. This enables users to distinguish and retrieve the proper card format for their device. Additional notes that link to an online user guide or describe other product information is also helpful for users. Finally, when using a multiple record approach, adding a note that relates the resource to other available formats–whether print, online or another expansion card–ensures the effective integration of all formats into the catalogue.

An emerging technology raises further challenges when describing the item. No cataloguing copy was found for PDA books on expansion cards in the major bibliographic utilities, so original records had to be created without the guidance of best practices. The *Anglo-American Cataloguing Rules* do not give explicit instructions for describing PDA cards in the physical description area of a record. General terms such as "computer chip cartridge" or "computer card" are suggested in chapter nine, but the rules now allow for the use of more conventional terminology as well. Among such terms are "expansion card," "extension card," "multi media card," or "memory card." "PDA expansion card" was finally chosen to describe the resource, as it is relevant for all models, but is not limited to any particular model's terminology.

Another challenge is how to package the resource. Since the cards themselves are the size of a print book's spine label, they cannot be labeled, shelved or retrieved effectively on their own. The practice at the University of Alberta Libraries is to insert the card into the pocket of a plastic sheet, which is then fastened inside a report cover. The labels are then attached to this cover. This standard size allows the cards to be integrated and shelved with other formats in the collection. Unfortunately, the size of the cards also prohibits them from being marked with any security provisions such as tattle tape, so they are still vulnerable to theft. The University of Alberta Libraries' PDA books are currently kept in the reserve collection with a two-week loan period, where they can be monitored more closely both for security and circulation reasons.

EXISTING LIBRARY RESOURCES
BECOME PDA-ACCESSIBLE

Implementing PDA-accessible collection services does not necessarily require the purchase or licensing of resources. Many existing library resources are accessible on PDA devices either through native PDA software applications or via the addition of free second-party software applications. To integrate existing collections and services in a PDA services model, librarians need to become familiar with PDA applications, be aware of how their patrons are using the devices, and promote the multi-format accessibility of library resources.

Transferring catalogue and database search results to a PDA, either though a desktop synchronization or an in-library infrared device, easily allows users to store and access small bits of information in a useful format for locating the material in the collection or for producing bibliographies at a later date. Reading and transporting documents in portable document format (PDF) using the free Adobe Acrobat Reader for mobile devices <http://www.adobe.com/products/acrobat/acrrmobiledevices. html> expands a library's e-journal collection into a PDA-accessible format. While the PDF format is not ideal for all documents, particularly articles with graphs or images that do not transfer well to the smaller screen, having the document text available for reading or referral on an any-time basis is a key feature of having a PDA. Many free e-books are also PDA accessible. High profile services such as the 1,800+ publicly-available e-books at the Electronic Text Center of the University of Virginia <http://etext.lib.Virginia.edu/uvaonline.html> and the e-book titles from Project Gutenberg <http://www.gutenberg. net/> offer free content that is PDA-accessible.

Web-clipping services, such as the popular AvantGo, allow patrons to select Web information as "custom channels" that allow monitoring of regularly updated Web services such as table-of-content pages of favorite journals, Weblogs or news services. Free software such as the IE2PDB IE5 Explorer Bar <http://pdacentral.ozbytes.net.au/palm/preview/ 173091.html>, Fling It <http://www.freewarepalm.com/communication/ flingit.shtml>, or Plucker <http://pdacentral.ozbytes.net.au/palm/preview/ 173091.html> let Palm OS users select the text of a Web page and transfer it onto their PDA. This is useful for information that changes infrequently such as library phone numbers and contact information, online bibliographies, or subject resource guides. Another way to integrate PDA resources into your library collection is with the development of in-house content. Most libraries have Websites with news items, resource guides, new book lists and more. Much of this Web content can easily be modified for use on a PDA and allow users easy any-time access to information about the library.

CONCLUSION

It is too early to gauge the success of library PDA services and PDA-specific collections and resources. Libraries are still in the early stages of implementation of such services. Licensing models are still evolving and library policies for best methods of practice are just beginning to be developed. Implementation will affect all areas of collections and acquisitions service, as well as reference and instruction. Accommodating the needs of your library's PDA users does not require an overwhelming commitment of time or money. Start simple, evaluate users' needs, and expand services as required in order to extend improved collections access to users.

SELECTED RESOURCES

Bridges, Karl. "Thoughts on the Future of Library Computing: Implications of the Use of Handheld Computers for Library Service." *Library Philosophy and Practice* 5:1 (2003): 1-7.

Fox, Megan K. *PDAs and Handhelds in Libraries and Academia: How the Academic Library Is Using PDA Technologies: Resources and Sample Projects.* Simmons College Libraries. <http://Web.simmons.edu/~fox/PDA.html>.

Galganski, Carol, Tom Peters, and Lori Bell. "Exploring Planet PDA." *Computers in Libraries* 22:9 (2002): 32-36.

Guide to Selecting a Personal Digital Assistant. University of Illinois at Chicago. University Library. <http://www.uic.edu/depts/lib/lhsp/temp/buying.pdf>.

Handheld Users Guide. University of Georgia Libraries. <http://www.libs.uga.edu/pda/>.

Heisey, Laura, and Michelle Paolillo. *Final Report: Beam-using Possibilities.* <http://www.library.cornell.edu/EMPSL/PDA-pilot-report.pdf>.

John, Nancy R., and Dennis C. Tucker. "10 Myths About PDAS–Debunked!" *Computers in Libraries* 23:3 (2003): 26-30.

Library of the Health Sciences Peoria. *Handspring Visors for Checkout.* <http://www.uic.edu/depts/lib/lhsp/temp/visors.pdf>.

PDA Applications. Health Sciences Library System. University of Pittsburgh and UPMC Health System. <http://www.hsls.pitt.edu/guides/pda/topics>.

PDA Applications at the UAMS Library. University of Arkansas for Medical Sciences. UAMS Library. <http://www.library.uams.edu/lrc/pdainfo/pdalibrary.htm>.

PDA Bibliography. UTHSCSA Library. University of Texas Health Science Center at San Antonio. <http://www.library.uthscsa.edu/Internet/PDAbibliography.cfm>.

PDA Books on Expansion/MultiMedia Cards. University of Alberta Libraries. <http://www.library.ualberta.ca/pdazone/books/index.cfm>.

PDA Fair 2002. Norris Medical Library. University of Southern California. <http://www.usc.edu/hsc/nml/spotlight/pda-fair-2002/index.html>.

PDA Hardware Reviews/Buying Tips. Harvey Cushing/John Hay Whitney Medical Library. Yale University. <http://www.med.yale.edu/library/reference/training/pda.html>.

PDA Information: Palm OS Syncing Station Guide. Himmelfarb Health Sciences Library. George Washington University Medical Center. <http://www.gwumc.edu/library/pdares/clarinet_palm.htm>.

PDA Information: Pocket PC OS Syncing Station Guide. Himmelfarb Health Sciences Library. George Washington University Medical Center. <http://www.gwumc.edu/library/pdares/clarinet_pc.htm>.

PDA Library Resources. University of Alberta Libraries. <http://www.library.ualberta.ca/pdazone/index.cfm>.

PDA Resources. UTHSCSA Library. University of Texas Health Science Center at San Antonio. <http://www.library.uthscsa.edu/Internet/pda.cfm>.

PDA Support. OSF Saint Francis Medical Center Library & Resource Center. <http://library.osfsaintfrancis.org/pda.htm>.

PDA Tutorial. Duke University Medical Center Library. <http://www.mclibrary.duke.edu/respub/guides/pdatutorial/>.

PDAZone. University of Alberta Libraries. <http://www.library.ualberta.ca/pdazone/index.cfm>.

Personal Digital Assistants for the Health Sciences: Other Library Sites. Hardin Library for the Health Sciences. The University of Iowa Libraries. <http://www.lib.uiowa.edu/hardin/pda/libraries.html>.

Personal Digital Assistants (PDA) Bibliography. Virginia Commonwealth University Libraries. <http://www.library.vcu.edu/tml/bibs/pdabibliography.html>.

Personal Digital Assistants (PDAs) Focus On Guide. Health Sciences Library. UNC–Chapel Hill. <http://www.hsl.unc.edu/guides/focusonpda.cfm>.

Ross, Theresa A. "Today's PDAs Can Put an OPAC in the Palm of Your Hand." *Computers in Libraries* 22:3 (2002): 14-22.

Schuyler, Michael. "The Next Big Thing: Super-PDAs Do It All." *Computers in Libraries* 22:6 (2002): 28-29.

Shipman, Jean P., and Andrew C. Morton. "The New Black Bag: PDAs, Health Care and Library Services." *Reference Services Review* 29:3 (2001): 229-37.

Smith, Russell. "Adapting a New Technology to the Academic Medical Library: Personal Digital Assistants." *Journal of the Medical Library Association* 90:1 (2002): 93-94.

Stoddard, Mari. *Health Care Journal Articles: The PDA Bibliography.* Arizona Health Sciences Library. <http://educ.ahsl.arizona.edu/pda/art.htm>.

Stoddard, Mari J. "Handhelds in the Health Sciences Library at the University of Arizona." *Medical Reference Services Quarterly* 20:3 (2001): 75-82.

Tutorials. UTHSCSA Library. University of Texas Health Science Center at San Antonio. <http://www.library.uthscsa.edu/consultation/guides/tutorials/>.

<untitled>. Western Kentucky University. <http://www.wku.edu/Library/tip/pda/index.htm>.

VCU Libraries To Go. Virginia Commonwealth University Libraries. <http://www.library.vcu.edu/pda/librarychannelinstructions.html>.

Welcome to LTLS PDA Connect. Lincoln Trail Libraries System. <http://www.ltls.org/pda.html>.

Which PDA Do I Buy? University of Virginia Health Sciences Library. <http://hsc.virginia.edu/hs-library/pda/whichone.html>.

Workshop Descriptions. Palms and Other PDAs: Beyond the Basics. Norris Medical Library. University of Southern California. <http://www.usc.edu/hsc/nml/lis/w-descriptions.html#palmpilots>.

Issues in the Development of an All-Digital Public Health Library in Michigan: The Michigan Community Health Electronic Library

Harvey R. Brenneise

SUMMARY. The Michigan Community Health Electronic Library (MCHEL) serves the public health and other community health workers in Michigan. It is committed to desktop delivery of the best health information to its primary clientele, with as much as possible in digital full-text form. It collaborates with other libraries in the state to make this possible. It is committed to full access to digital information resources from its integrated library system, and seeks to market its services to the primary clientele as well as to train them. *[Article copies available for a fee from The Haworth Document Delivery Service: 1-800-HAWORTH. E-mail address: <docdelivery@haworthpress.com> Website: <http://www.HaworthPress.com> © 2005 by The Haworth Press, Inc. All rights reserved.]*

KEYWORDS. Public health libraries, collection development, World Wide Web, library consortia

Harvey R. Brenneise is Library Director, Michigan Community Health Electronic Library, Michigan Public Health Institute, 2436 Woodlake Circle, Okemos, MI 48864 (E-mail: hbrenne@mphi.org).

[Haworth co-indexing entry note]: "Issues in the Development of an All-Digital Public Health Library in Michigan: The Michigan Community Health Electronic Library." Brenneise, Harvey R. Co-published simultaneously in *The Acquisitions Librarian* (The Haworth Information Press, an imprint of The Haworth Press, Inc.) No. 33/34, 2005, pp. 147-157; and: *Managing Digital Resources in Libraries* (ed: Audrey Fenner) The Haworth Information Press, an imprint of The Haworth Press, Inc., 2005, pp. 147-157. Single or multiple copies of this article are available for a fee from The Haworth Document Delivery Service [1-800-HAWORTH, 9:00 a.m. - 5:00 p.m. (EST). E-mail address: docdelivery@haworthpress.com].

Digital Object Identifier: 10.1300/J101v17n33_13

HISTORY

The Michigan Community Health Electronic Library (MCHEL) <http://www.mchel.org> was born in March 1998 as part of a plan to migrate the state's "mostly print" community health library resources, consisting of five existing print libraries, to a virtual "mostly digital" library available to authorized community health users across the state. The five libraries are the Michigan Dept. of Community Health Library (formerly the Dept. of Public Health Library, established in 1873), the Michigan Public Health Institute Library, and libraries at three mental health facilities in the greater Detroit area.

In 1996 former Governor John Engler "streamlined" state government by consolidating public health, mental health, aging, Medicare and Medicaid departments and agencies into a new "super-department" called the Dept. of Community Health (MDCH). Also during the Engler administration (1990), legislation was passed establishing the Michigan Public Health Institute (MPHI) as a not-for-profit agency to serve state government through non-competitive contracts with state departments, primarily but not exclusively MDCH <http://www.mphi.org>.

One of the contracts awarded MPHI was development of a digital library to serve the entire consolidated department and its state, regional and local affiliates. The first task was to hire a library director, which was done early in 1998. An initial task was to create policies and manage the processes of this new entity, including collaborating with the existing print libraries in the department in making resources available to the newly expanded clientele.

VISION

In addition to limited funding, the primary challenge historically for a state public health library was serving a clientele that is widely distributed geographically. Most state employees are based in the state capital of Lansing, working in buildings scattered around the city in various locations. In addition, there are 43 local health departments in counties or groups of counties (only one, Detroit, has a library), local Community Mental Health (CMH) facilities, and various other local and regional providers of community health services. In the past, these remote users had very limited access to the print library, usually no more than an occasional phone question or interlibrary loan request. The availability of digital resources created an opportunity to better serve the entire clientele now that information resources are no longer geographically limited in the way paper-based libraries are. However, a new vision and paradigm were required to take advantage of this new reality.

One of the first tasks of the new library director, working with a small advisory committee, was the development of a vision statement, mission, goals and objectives, and a collection development policy to guide the development of the new digital library (MCHEL Vision <http://www.mchel.org/mchelmission.html>), adopted in September 1998. MCHEL's vision is to create and maintain "an integrated electronic health information delivery system for the Michigan health community and general public" and its mission is "is to effectively deliver appropriate health information to health professionals and the general public in Michigan to enhance quality of life." A critical change was made in its definition of primary clientele from the previous print library by the specific inclusion of information service to all divisions and units of the new MDCH rather than just "public health," as well as to non-MDCH community health organizations in Michigan such as MPHI, local health departments, other local community health agencies (such as CMH facilities) and other "allies" in the provision of community health services. At that time, it was estimated that there were approximately 6,000 MDCH employees as well as a similar number of employees of these "allied organizations," for a total of potential clientele of 12,000.

DEVELOPMENTAL STRATEGIES

The adopted goals and objectives, as modified over time, have provided the framework for development both of library services and collections. Because the print library did not have a catalog, acquisition of an integrated library system to manage all types of library resources, including electronic, was a primary objective. However, because of the length of time required to negotiate and implement such a system, the library director chose to develop a Web site as a temporary measure to highlight important resources, knowing that in time the database of such selected resources would be far too large to be easily handled from a Web page.

The collection development policy calls for selectively creating links to the most important free community health Web sites and publications. Particular emphasis is placed on Michigan resources, which will be "collected" comprehensively. Creating a Web page that contained these resources was a prime initial activity of the new digital library, with plans for cataloging and placing them into an integrated library system.

Another primary library objective is to ensure title-level electronic access to the maximum number of print subscriptions currently received at the library in Lansing, with later attention to be given to doing the same with the mental health collections in the Detroit area. The print library has a limited current subscription list of 93 titles (budget of $33,000). In addition, there are a number of government serial titles such as the *Morbidity and Mortality Weekly Report*, previously purchased in paper, which are now available electronically at no cost except for cataloging. These paper subscriptions have been cancelled. Of the 93 titles, in 2003 about 80% are available in an accessible electronic form.

Serials have always presented "control" problems to librarians–claiming, binding, etc. Simply locating and linking to the electronic resources was remarkably time-consuming, indicating that perhaps migrating to primarily electronic delivery has not, at least yet, resolved the need for significant staff resources to manage serial subscriptions. The subscription list still includes several that are free on the Web (raising the question of cancellation of the print subscription in tight economic times), some that are available through aggregators such as the American Psychological Association (PsycINFO Full Text), some from the serials vendor's Web site, and many more from the publisher's Web sites or Ingenta. A significant number are available from more than one site, often with different "start dates." A small number are only available through aggregators such as OVID and MDConsult which, because of cost, MCHEL users cannot access.

The library director contacted all editors of publications not currently available electronically and inquired about their future intentions to make them available in that format. Answers included plans to go online in the near future as well as a few "mom and pop" (or perhaps more accurately, "out of a single academician's office") publications that either do not believe they have the resources to go online or do not know the process of doing so. These may represent excellent potential for library/publisher collaboration, perhaps through grant funding if the results are made freely available on the Web. In addition, a JSTOR-like project for back issues of medical titles would be useful for the many space-pressed hospital libraries that would like to discard their paper copies but are unwilling to depend on interlibrary loan for access if they do so in the absence of digital access.

With an acquisitions budget of $20,000 for electronic resources, MCHEL has purchased the following subscription services to support activities of MDCH and MPHI: *Physicians' Desk Reference, Facts and Comparisons, Harrison's Principles of Internal Medicine, Cochrane Library* (evidence-based medicine), *Biblioline* (*AIDSearch* and *Child Abuse, Child Welfare & Adoption* database) and two grants resources: *Community of Science* and *Foundation Directory.*

COLLABORATION EFFORTS

One of the organizational goals of MPHI is to assist Michigan health organizations to collaborate more effectively in meeting common goals. In addition to MDCH, the University of Michigan, Michigan State University, and Wayne State University are the official sponsors of MPHI and have representatives on its board. Seeing the success of the OhioLINK program just across the state line and wanting to see if Michigan could apply the lessons learned there, MPHI convened a planning process of librarians representing all types of libraries called AccessMichigan Electronic Community Health Information Initiative (Brenneise and Marks <http://www.ifla.org/IV/ifla66/papers/009-153e.htm>). Unfortunately, the result from this process to date has been limited to the planning documents themselves <http://www.mchel.org/AMECHII/> and two unsuccessful grant proposals. Its intention of voluntarily pooling economic resources for the common good remains to be realized. Reasons for lack of more progress may include the lack of planning staff dedicated to the project and possibly the tendency of librarians to think institutionally in an information world that is increasingly becoming post-institutional.

Another MCHEL collaborative effort was a pilot project with the libraries at Michigan State University (MSU) to share their Innovative Interfaces Incorporated integrated library system, a system that MCHEL could not afford to purchase on its own. This enabled MCHEL for the first time to integrate all of its cataloging records (for print and electronic resources) into a single information portal. However, in January 2003 MSU librarians chose to terminate the project, reportedly because they found that the presence of cataloging records identifying resources not immediately available to their own users was confusing and not acceptable.

The most successful MCHEL collaborative ventures have been with hospital libraries, particularly the members of the Michigan Health Sciences Libraries Association (MHSLA) <http://www.mhsla.org>. One of the objectives of the AMECHII project was to complete one successful self-funded collaborative venture to use as an example and incentive for additional projects. Following the grant-writing axiom of "picking the low-hanging fruit first," the Stat!Ref <http://www.statref.com> suite of medical textbooks and reference materials (currently 44 titles) was chosen. It was a product that had a high level of interest among MHSLA libraries (mostly hospital and academic health science libraries), although some titles, such as the *Diagnostic and Statistical Manual of Mental Disorders* would be of wider interest.

Combining the peculiarities of Stat!Ref pricing, economies of scale, and flexibility within the group in the way costs to libraries are allocated, a win/win situation was created where all libraries from the largest to the smallest saved money, whether current subscribers or not. In addition, the group purchase allowed many more libraries (particularly the smaller ones) to purchase the product at a price they could afford. The pilot project was implemented October 1, 2001, and has already gone through one annual renewal cycle. No library has dropped out, and a number of libraries have joined during this period, making a total of 30 current subscribers. Inexplicably, at least two Michigan Stat!Ref subscribing libraries did not join the group purchase even though they would both have saved money had they done so.

The "Priceline model" of pricing has proven remarkably successful in distributing the costs, with enough additional funding to purchase new titles when they are released. The current contract is for 40 simultaneous users (flexibly shared among the group as a whole in any combination at a given moment). Individual libraries determine what it would cost to "go it alone" given their local needs, and on that basis offer to purchase *x* number of simultaneous users at the lower group rate. The maximum number of concurrent users has never been exceeded, although the vendor has agreed not to shut anyone out if this does occur. If it did, this will be taken into consideration in negotiating the following year's contract. It has been the experience both of the vendor and of this author that many libraries, especially when purchasing individually, "overbuy" when purchasing on the basis of simultaneous use, perhaps in an effort to ensure that no one is shut out, or perhaps with an unrealistic expectation of usage levels.

The second successful collaboration for collection development that came out of working with MHSLA libraries was the purchase of 754 NetLibrary e-book titles <http://www.mhsla.org/netlibrary.pdf> with grant funding from the National Library of Medicine (NLM). The Library of Michigan had previously purchased over 10,000 NetLibrary e-book titles with federal Library Services and Technology Act (LSTA) funding, and made them available free to all Michigan libraries as well as residents from home through the Michigan Electronic Library (MEL) program <http://www.mel.org>. The new NLM-funded titles were added to the MEL collection in March 2003 and made available to everyone in the state on the same basis as the previous titles. Titles include both consumer health and clinical titles, and represent many standard medical publishers.

In order to have a complete digital collection of Michigan community health documents, MCHEL has submitted a grant proposal to NLM to digitize the entire collection of print publications of MDCH and its antecedents. Research at the Lane Library at Stanford (Rindfleisch <http://smi-web.stanford.edu/people/tcr/tcr-hsl-futures.html>) concludes that like "bad money driving out good," the presence or expectation of digital resources tends to "drive out" patron usage of print ones. Like many other "collections" of government documents, these print resources are presently somewhat scattered, and digitizing them will "bring them together" again. Especially in public health, where longitudinal data are important if not essential, having the entire collection available in a single place, and deliverable to the desktop, will be a significant improvement over the current "scattershot" approach. For these, as for the electronic publications of MDCH and MPHI, grant funding was also sought for full OCLC MARC cataloging to prevent their becoming more digital "gray literature."

ACCESS ISSUES

It has often been said that using the World Wide Web is too often like "drinking from a fire hose." MCHEL is an effort to gather together the Michigan community health information in a more "drinkable" way. A presupposition is that users want a minimal number of information interfaces, one if possible. Because of its centrality to bibliographic access to biomedical literature, PubMed (MEDLINE) will, in a medical library, be one of these interfaces, so in this case the minimum number of interfaces is two. For PubMed, MCHEL will use the Linkout and Loansome Doc features to enhance ease of access. In harmony with its presupposition, MCHEL is designed as a unified interface in contrast with the approach taken by many libraries of having multiple Web pages for various formats and types of information resources. While specialized Web pages are sometimes useful as a method of guiding users to related resources, when too large or numerous they may become unmanageable, losing users in their complexity and/or overlooking important resources "hidden" in an aggregation.

This is particularly true with serials. Because of this presupposition, MCHEL catalogs all serial titles that are "held" in full text regardless of location (sometimes with a brief rather than full MARC record), including those found in aggregations such as PsycINFO, OCLC WilsonSelectPlus, Gale Health and Wellness Resource Center and Gale General Reference Center Gold. The latter three are received at no cost to the library through MEL, and titles are selected from the aggregations for cataloging based on the special collection interests of MCHEL. On occasion, multiple holdings statements are given when access is possible through more than one interface. In addition, serial titles from HighWire Press and other free titles have been added where they might be of interest, along with "holdings statements" that sometimes indicate that the current issues are not available. When a library is minimally funded, there is an advantage to access to information sources like these even when they are not complete. Efficient interlibrary loan is always available for articles that are not accessible free in full text.

In the case of Stat!Ref, cataloging consists of a single MARC record with multiple 505 |t fields for the titles it contains, along with alternate titles that might be more familiar to a medical clientele. What is lost through this approach, of course, is the individual subject indexing and other useful data that a user might find when searching by other than title.

Part of the agreement with OCLC and the Michigan Library Consortium for the Net!Library purchase included a free set of OCLC MARC records for each title in the collection for any library in the state that desires it. In addition, a second OCLC collection set is being created of the medical titles (including other medical library interests such as psychology, computer books and management titles) so that health libraries in the state can add these to their catalogs as well, without either having to select over 1,000 titles individually and download them from OCLC or accept the full set of over 10,000 titles that includes any that are irrelevant to a special collection. Including these in the integrated library system will simplify user searches, as well as make these resources more readily available.

In the future, libraries or groups of libraries may find it useful to create other OCLC MARC collection sets of free selected resources in specialized areas such as medicine or public health (for example, for public health libraries, electronic resources of the Centers for Disease Control and Prevention). Implementing a product like SFX may also increase access to digital resources by all users. The Clinical Digital Libraries Project <http://www.slis.ua.edu/dls/cdlp/> is of considerable interest, as among other things, it makes access to chapter level information (for example, in medical textbooks) available through the integrated library system.

TRAINING AND MARKETING

With only a single librarian at MCHEL and a library paraprofessional at MDCH, the amount of time "left" for these activities is limited indeed, and yet the needs and opportunities are great, including the many potential users who have never had access to a library of this magnitude before. Members of a focus group held in East Lansing in March 2003 clearly indicated that extensive training is needed in all 43 of the local health departments which includes many types of users, but in particular community health nurses. Fortunately, *CINAHL* is one of the free databases available through MEL.

"Getting the word out" to all the potential users is also a very large task, considering that the user group consists of more than 10,000 people in a wide variety of disciplines. To date, most of the publicity has been done in a biweekly column called "LibraryLinks" in the MDCH newsletter *News Briefs* that goes to each employee with his paycheck. Marketing efforts to the local departments and allied organizations will be increased. Grant funding will also be sought to meet the additional needs for training and marketing.

THE FUTURE

Future plans and projects of MCHEL include the following:

- Complete the virtual merger of electronic resources within MDCH as part of the "bureaucracy buster" program of Gov. Jennifer Granholm, giving better access to more people at a lower cost, at state and local levels.
- Complete the installation of an Ariel server to expedite the desktop delivery of interlibrary loans.

- Complete the installation of an EZ-Proxy server for patron authentication of remote users.
- In concert with other Michigan libraries, particularly at the hospitals, purchase electronic journals from publishers as a "pooled resource" on the OhioLINK model (also used in several European countries) so that all libraries have access to all the publications of a given publisher (the so-called "big deal").
- Explore the possibility of a shared virtual reference service with other health libraries in Michigan, and potentially around the world, making 24x7 reference service available.
- Explore the possibility of developing specialized health resources for population groups in Michigan along the MedlinePlus model–for example, the Arabic-speaking population in the Detroit area.
- Seek other collaborative partners such as public health institutes in other states or small libraries in Michigan with limited library service.

CONCLUSION

The Michigan Community Health Electronic Library is committed to making health information available to its various clienteles where and when it is needed. Because the public health depends on complete and accurate information to all clinicians and the general public, this is a public health imperative.

REFERENCES

AccessMichigan Electronic Community Health Information Initiative (AMECHII): Final Documents. 4 April 2003. <http://www.mchel.org/AMECHII/>.

Brenneise, Harvey R. and Ellen B. Marks. "Creating a State-wide Health Library: The Michigan Experience." *Proceedings of the International Federation of Library Associations, 2002*, pp. 7-12. 4 April 2003. <http://www.ifla.org/IV/ifla66/papers/009-153e.htm>.

Health Sciences Titles Added to the MeL NetLibrary Collection: March 2003. 4 April 2003. <http://www.mhsla.org/netlibrary.pdf>.

MCHEL Vision, Mission, Goals and Objectives, and Collection Development Policy. 4 April 2003. <http://www.mchel.org/mchelmission.html>.

Michigan Community Health Electronic Library. 4 April 2003. <http://www.mchel.org>.

Michigan Health Sciences Libraries Association. 4 April 2003. <http://www.mhsla.org/>.

Michigan Public Health Institute. 4 April 2003. <http://www.mphi.org>.

Rindfleisch, Thomas C. "W(h)ither Health Sciences Libraries: Preliminary Study of the Dynamics and Effects of Digital Materials Use on the Future Roles of Health Science Libraries, Sept. 17, 2001." 4 April 2003. <http://smi-web.stanford.edu/ people/tcr/tcr-hsl-futures.html>.

Stat!Ref Electronic Medical Library. 4 April 2003. <http://www.statref.com/>.

Welcome to the Clinical Digital Libraries Project. 4 April 2003. <http://www.slis.ua. edu/dls/cdlp/>.

Welcome to the Michigan eLibrary. 4 April 2003. <http://www.mel.org>.

Electronic Collection Management: Completing the Cycle– Experiences at Two Libraries

Judith Hiott

Carla Beasley

SUMMARY. The development of the Internet and the online collections accessed by it has created major adjustments in all library functions, including collection management and budgeting. The authors share how two public libraries have come full circle in electronic collection management, beginning with early selection, followed by current weeding programs and developing plans for future collections. *[Article copies available for a fee from The Haworth Document Delivery Service: 1-800-HAWORTH. E-mail address: <docdelivery@haworthpress.com> Website: <http://www.HaworthPress.com> © 2005 by The Haworth Press, Inc. All rights reserved.]*

KEYWORDS. Online resources, electronic collection development, integration of print and digital resources

---

Judith Hiott is Assistant Coordinator of Materials Selection, Houston Public Library, Houston, TX (E-mail: judith.hiott@cityofhouston.net). Carla Beasley is Assistant Director for Materials Services, Forsyth County Public Library, Cumming, GA (E-mail: beasleyc@mail.forsyth.public.lib.ga.us).

[Haworth co-indexing entry note]: "Electronic Collection Management: Completing the Cycle–Experiences at Two Libraries." Hiott, Judith, and Carla Beasley. Co-published simultaneously in *The Acquisitions Librarian* (The Haworth Information Press, an imprint of The Haworth Press, Inc.) No. 33/34, 2005, pp. 159-178; and: *Managing Digital Resources in Libraries* (ed: Audrey Fenner) The Haworth Information Press, an imprint of The Haworth Press, Inc., 2005, pp. 159-178. Single or multiple copies of this article are available for a fee from The Haworth Document Delivery Service [1-800-HAWORTH, 9:00 a.m. - 5:00 p.m. (EST). E-mail address: docdelivery@haworthpress.com].

Digital Object Identifier: 10.1300/J101v17n33_14

Collection management staff who have seen robust budgets in the last five years are now preparing for hard times. During a time of economic prosperity, acquisitions departments fattened existing print collections and started online collections. Vendors scrambled to convert their popular print sources into licensed electronic products, and libraries built digital collections to reach beyond their walls to home and business users remotely. It was a small renaissance in library collection development.

With the downturn of the economy, library budgets are being reduced, and materials budgets are not exempt. Librarians from two public libraries, Houston Public Library and Forsyth County Public Library, discuss how their electronic collections sprouted, grew, and are now being pruned.

THE LIBRARIES

The Houston Public Library (HPL) will be 100 years old in 2004. In that time a single downtown branch serving a population of about 66,000 has become a network of 37 branches serving an extremely diverse population of 1.9 million, the fourth largest city in the United States. The business base, heavily dependent on the energy industry in the eighties, has seen diversification with rapid growth in sectors such as engineering services, health services and manufacturing. Currently a Central Library downtown re-examines its research role in preparation for an upcoming renovation and reorganization. Four large district branches and 32 neighborhood branches struggle to provide traditional and new services in mostly "booming" establishments.

Forsyth County Public Library (FCPL) celebrated its seventh anniversary as an independent county system on July 1, 2003. Records indicate that there was some library service in Forsyth County in the 1920s. "Aunt Laura" Hockenhull had a private library where young and old could mingle and browse among the books. In 1938, the first formal Forsyth County Public Library was established by the Works Progress Administration with 600 volumes. In 1959, Forsyth County Public Library joined a three-county regional system, which resulted in a new, 25,000 square foot building opening in 1992. With high population growth and increased local funding, FCPL again became an independent county system on July 1, 1996. Over the next few years, administrative staff was added and a second county branch opened in November 2000.

Forsyth County lies at the edge of the Greater Atlanta Metropolitan area, and has been one of the top three fastest-growing counties in the United States since 1997. Population grew from 44,000 in 1990 to over 110,000 in 2002 (U.S. Census). Once primarily a rural, agrarian economy fueled by the poultry industry, Forsyth County is evolving into a white-collar business culture, with 60% of the work force commuting outside of the county to work, according to the Forsyth County Chamber of Commerce. Table 1 compares services and features of both libraries.

ADVENT OF ONLINE

Houston Public Library's online collection began in the late 1980s with a small collection of CD-ROM indexes at the Central Library. A collection of periodical articles accessible via a dial-up line followed in the early 1990s. These collections were among the library's first subscription offerings on the Internet and became the core of the Internet collection. As other products became available, the library chose additional databases and beginning in 1994, the Texas State Library purchased databases for a public library consortium, the Texas State Electronic Library (TSEL). The 1999 merger of TSEL with the State Library's academic library consortium TexShare increased the purchasing power of both consortia. The merger resulted in a number of HPL's individual subscriptions being taken over by the state, freeing over $200,000 to buy additional databases. Currently, TexShare provides in-house and remote access to 94 databases. HPL provides in-house and remote access to 37 databases and in-house use only to one database. Databases paid for from the Houston Public Library budget are shown in Table 2.

TABLE 1. Library Statistics for Comparison Purposes

Statistic	HPL	FCPL
Service area population	1,953,631	117,139
Cardholders	499,630	45,523
Number of branches + main	37	2
Circulation (FY02)	6,085,583	1,058,163
Holdings	4,713,879	209,273
Number of licensed databases purchased by the library	32	19
Materials Budget (FY03)	$5,700,000	$432,992
Percent of budget for electronic	8.20%	11.50%

TABLE 2. Houston Public Library FY03 Database Subscriptions

Name	Vendor	Access
AP Photo Archive	Accunet/AP	Remote
Ancestry Plus	Gale	In Library Only
Biography Resource Center	Gale	Remote
CollegeSource	Career Guidance Foundation	Remote
Ready Reference Shelf	Gale	Remote
Grove Dictionary of Art	Oxford University Press	Remote
Grove Dictionary of Music	Oxford University Press	Remote
Historical NY Times	ProQuest	Remote
History Resource Center-US	Gale	Remote
History Resource Center-Modern World	Gale	Remote
General Reference Center Gold	Gale	Remote
Investext	Gale	Remote
Learn-A-Test	Learning Express	Remote
Congressional Universe	Lexis-Nexis	Remote
Mergent FISonline	Mergent	Remote
Newsbank Houston Chronicle	Newsbank	Remote
Newsbank Texas Newsfile	Newsbank	Remote
Novelist	EBSCO	Remote
Electronic Collections Online	OCLC FirstSearch	Remote
Business and Management Practices	OCLC FirstSearch	Remote
Periodical Abstracts	OCLC FirstSearch	Remote
Facts on File	OCLC FirstSearch	Remote
Wilson Select Plus	OCLC FirstSearch	Remote
MLA Bibliography	OCLC FirstSearch	Remote
OED Online	Oxford University Press	Remote
Opposing Viewpoints (Gale)	Gale	Remote
Physicians Desk Reference	Micromedex, Inc.	Remote
Poem Finder	Roth Publishing	Remote
Reader's Guide Retrospective	Wilson	Remote
Reference USA	InfoUSA	Remote
Serials Solutions	Serials Solutions	Remote
Statistical Universe	Lexis-Nexis	Remote
Sybworld	Macmillan	Remote
World Book Online	World Book	Remote

Forsyth County Public Library inherited CD-ROM database products from its previous association with the regional system. In 1996, FCPL had *ProQuest, American Business Disk, SIRS*, and *Facts on File*. The CD-ROM products represented a huge accumulation of information in one place, more than the library could imagine purchasing at one time. Fees were high, but not impossible to justify, given the amount of data.

In 1998, the State of Georgia Board of Regents introduced GALILEO, GeorgiA LIbrary LEarning Online, a virtual library of licensed databases and Internet research sites. Like Houston Public Library's TexShare, GALILEO provided access to many of the products FCPL had paid for, allowing FCPL to regain almost half of the budget for electronic products from local dollars. With this money, FCPL moved beyond server-run CD-ROMs, and licensed new databases provided through Internet access. These were chosen primarily on their availability and overall appeal. With prosperity still on the doorstep, it was as much a question of "What's out there to buy" as of traditional collection development.

EXPANDING ONLINE RESOURCES

As the market expanded and more electronic resources became available, Houston Public Library looked for products that had the kind of information that users demanded in print. In addition, the database vendors had to validate by IP address, and the databases had to be compatible with library hardware. Finally, the products had to be easy to use, have online features that made them preferable to print counterparts, and upon trial be highly recommended by at least two reference staff. As with books, vendor negotiations and database reviews are managed in the library's Office of Materials Selection. This is reflected in the 2001 revision to the HPL Materials Selection Policy. Occasionally a user calls or e-mails the library to suggest a database. Every effort is made to comply with these requests if other criteria are met.

Management established a guideline early in the process that all online products would be purchased system-wide and preferably be available remotely because availability "wherever, whenever" was an inherent advantage of the format. Databases that might otherwise have been purchased were not because pricing models for large populations and multiple buildings made the cost too high for the expected use. To their credit, many vendors have been flexible. Several permitted remote use after a year or two of in-house use when concerns about data theft and/or erosion of the consumer market proved unfounded. With availability of excellent usage statistics, some vendors are showing signs of being willing to license at a reduced level the first year with pricing the following years based on an agreed cost per use.

Forsyth County Public Library began to plan and structure electronic resources within its collection development strategy in 2000. As part of the process of opening a new branch, FCPL added a Web page and remote patron authentication for licensed Internet products. Additional materials funding was available from the building project, and this was added to a portion of the print reference funds that were reallocated for electronic reference.

To decide how to approach incorporating electronic formats into the system collection, staff relied on information from *Building Electronic Library Collections* by Diane Kovacs. The author states that:

> Collection development of Internet resources for a Web-based e-library can be based on the same basic collection policy as traditional resources. Most libraries have devoted considerable time to developing collections of materials that best serve their communities of clients. (Kovacs, 2)

FCPL decided that the existing Materials Management Policy offered sufficient selection criteria for electronic products, and no additional Electronic Collection Development Policy was written. The selector for print reference assumed the task of electronic reference. In selecting the core, high demand areas of print reference and nonfiction–homework resources, medicine, business, and consumer research–were identified. As in print selection, reviews in professional publications guided selection, although reviews were hard to find. Remote access was important, and electronic products with remote licensing were preferred.

Seven new databases were added by the fall of 2000, forming a "core" electronic collection. By the end of 2002, FCPL's electronic collection consisted of the licensed databases shown in Table 3.

Another decision made in 2000 was to add free links to the catalog. The selection guideline stated that an Internet site would be cataloged if the site duplicated a resource currently in print. Now FCPL did not have to own the print. For example, *Kelley Blue Book* was added as a link. FCPL gets *NADA* in print. About 60 sites are currently cataloged. They are given a regular Dewey number, with a "WR" prefix (Web Refer-

TABLE 3. FCPL Premium Databases

Title	Vendor	Access
American Indian History and Culture	Facts on File	Remote
Business & Company Resource Center	Gale	Remote
Career Guidance Online	Facts on File	Remote
Consumer Reports Online	Consumer Reports	In Library Only
Countrywatch	Countrywatch	Remote
Facts.com	Facts on File News Service	Remote
Health and Wellness Resource Center	Gale	Remote
Hoover's Online	Hoover's	In Library Only
Literature Resource Center	Gale	Remote
Poem Finder	Roth	Remote
Ready Reference Shelf	Gale	Remote
Reference USA	InfoUSA	Remote
Science Experiments Online	Facts on File	Remote
Atlanta Journal-Constitution Stacks	Newsbank	In Library Only
Student Resource Center Gold	Gale	Remote
What Do I Read Next?	Gale	Remote
Wilson Biographies Plus Illustrated	H. W. Wilson	Remote
World Book Online	World Book	Remote
Wall Street Journal Online	Wall Street Journal	In Library Only

ence). The policy was updated recently to include links that contain similar information to print sources, such as biography.com and Firstgov.com.

An abridged display page of WR sites in the public catalog is shown in Table 4.

BEGINNING TO WEED

The existence of TexShare and GALILEO, along with a booming economy, gave the luxury of an excellent budget for about four years. This helped both Houston Public Library and Forsyth County Public Library begin the transition from mostly paper resources to the beginnings of a well-honed print and online collection. However, online reference sources changed budget priorities. Online sources were a great deal more expensive than traditional print. Even with the existence of TexShare, the HPL online materials budget has fluctuated between $400,000 and $450,000 for most of its history. Currently, the $467,000 online budget represents 8.2% of the total materials budget. FCPL spent

TABLE 4. FCPL Cataloged Web Reference Sites

Call Number	Title	Author
WR 292.13 BULFI	Bulfinch's mythology [Web site]	Bulfinch, Thomas, 1796-1867
WR 312.9 GEORG	Georgia vital statistics report online [Web site]	
WR 317.3 AMERI	American FactFinder [Web site]	United States. Bureau of the Census
WR 328.738 UNITE	Congressional directory [Web site]	United States. Congress.
WR 343.7305 IRS	IRS forms [Web site]	U.S. Department of the Treasury
WR 616.024 MERCK	The Merck manual of health information –home edition [Web site]	

over $46,000 on licensed public databases in fiscal year 2002, 11.5% of the total materials budget.

Chart 1 illustrates how expenditures for online databases have increased for FCPL.

While budgets were increasing each year, current licenses could be maintained, even with renewal increases, and new databases added. When budgets became static, or worse, reduced, both print and electronic collections had to be scrutinized. Budget line reallocation, alternative sources of funding, and state consortia electronic libraries did not provide necessary funds. Both libraries entered the third stage of a collection management cycle–weeding.

Houston's and Forsyth's experiences reflect a trend around the country, as seen in a recent article from *Library Journal* about its annual book-buying survey of public libraries:

> This year, [. . .] librarians are compelled as never before to make some hardheaded decisions regarding books purchases. They are taking various approaches to this challenge, from cutting back on multiple copies and standing orders to buying more paperbacks. (Hoffert, 42)

To address budget shifts in print and online, and to establish a fiscally defensible balance between formats, both libraries incorporated several guiding principles.

First, some portion of the print collection had to be replaced by online equivalents or not purchased in order to purchase the online collection. Duplicate purchases between print and electronic formats, as well as within the same format, had to be justified or eliminated.

CHART 1. FCPL Expenditures for Electronic Resources

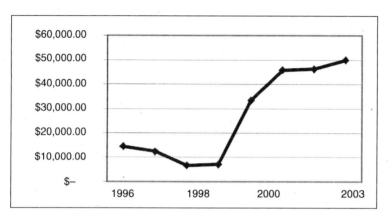

Second, the transition from print to electronic format and the weed-ing of both print and electronic titles had to be gradual. Small, inex-pensive pilot projects preceded larger replacement efforts so that a significant number of staff and users adjusted to the changes as they happened.

Third, weeding practices for the electronic collection had to be consistent with established procedures for weeding print and other non-electronic media. Factors including usage data, public demand, fo-cus on primary services, and staff input had to support changes.

IMPLEMENTATION OF WEEDING GUIDELINES

Three collections were targeted for transitional weeding projects: periodicals, reference materials, and e-books. Although both libraries incorporated the three guiding principles listed above, system size, overall budget, and user communities required that each library take a slightly different approach to implementation.

Periodicals

Although the public embraced online periodical services immedi-ately, Houston Public Library took more than three years to begin heavy cuts to the print collection. A few early aggregated periodicals databases reduced the retrieval of print periodicals at HPL's branches to almost none in a short time. Branch librarians needed less than a nod to replace the stodgier print titles previously essential to homework assignments with the hottest print newsstand titles on the market. Circulating back issues became a logical progression of this change–making branch print periodical collections extremely popular.

The Central Library periodical collection contains about 2,000 print titles to support research up to sophomore college level as well as the business community. A monthly count of print periodical retrievals at the Central Library revealed a 70% decrease over a seven-year period after aggregated periodicals databases were purchased. While it was clear that HPL would eventually drop low-use periodicals in this collection, the library started with several smaller steps. For three years, HPL spent less than $10,000 annually for access to e-journals for existing print titles when the cost to add online was free or minimal. The current collection has 272 e-journal titles. Users access these through the OCLC Firstsearch's *Electronic Collections Online* database. Next, HPL subscribed to the Serials Solutions service that tracks the full-text online periodical content of the aggregated database and e-journal subscriptions and presents the results in a title list. Finally, with the help of a summer intern from Rice University, the library developed a Web-based retrieval system that automated the collection of data about print periodical retrievals at a title level.

All of these initiatives were designed to provide data for the fiscal year 2004 periodicals drop/add cycle. With the expectation of a 20% materials budget cut in fiscal year 2004, all locations were asked to decrease their periodicals collections by 20%. It was recommended that the Central Library's periodicals collection be cut by 30%. The effort was thoughtful and often agonizing to the participating staff, but total cuts reached $330,000. Nonetheless, the cuts reflected changes in the reference emphasis throughout the system due to the existence of the Internet and a decrease in in-house reference use at Central. A third of the total drops were not from the traditional print collection. They included daily subscriptions to newspapers from around the country and the world, a 25% cut in CD-ROM standards subscriptions, a CD-ROM service of SEC filings and annual reports, and a congressional hearing service on microfilm. Print journals that were dropped at Central generally fell in two categories: expensive academic titles such as *Behavioral Neuroscience* and extra copies of titles previously needed to ensure a bindery copy. Most of the titles in the latter category are popular enough to buy in print, but with online access to these journals, the print copies on the open shelf remain in acceptable condition to bind. As the budget improves, HPL hopes to purchase bundles of e-journals from vendors such as the American Psychological Association, Project MUSE and J-Stor in lieu of dropped print titles.

Forsyth County Public Library's periodical collection differs greatly from Houston's Central Library collection. With only two branches, space is very limited for magazine display shelving, and there is no room for storage. Just over 200 titles are ordered each year, giving each branch about 170 adult, teen, juvenile, and easy-reading-level magazine subscriptions. Back issues are kept for two years, and all issues except the current one circulate three weeks, the same as books and media. Support for Kindergarten through Grade 12 students is usually satisfied through GALILEO. Post-secondary studies that cannot be supported through GALILEO are handled through Interlibrary Loan.

Six years ago it was vital to subscribe to magazines focusing on current events, politics, business, and the economy. Print periodical renewals were handled under a "drop/add" system to maintain space limitations, but funds were flexible to allow for renewal increases.

Then GALILEO brought EBSCOhost and ProQuest periodicals to the public, school, and academic libraries, as well as remotely to home users. Beginning in 2001, FCPL dropped several subscriptions that had been part of the traditional print collection, including *U.S. News & World Report, Economist, Kiplinger's Personal Finance*, and *Psychology Today*. In 2002, budget cuts required that more periodicals were dropped than were added. *Forbes, Mutual Funds, Business Week, Harvard Business Review*, and other titles were canceled. Home decorating, crafts, and fashion magazines led the circulation figures.

The selection of magazines has now evolved to a browsing, popular collection, with renewals dependent on usage. Other libraries cite a similar trend in selection policies:

> "Our collection development has been refocused toward supplying more popular materials vs. scholarly or reference titles," notes Tom Horne of the Seattle PL, where circulation has soared ten percent. At the Manchester PL, CT, says Ramona Harten, "We've done a better job of selecting materials to satisfy demand." (Hoffert, 43)

At FCPL, new subscriptions will have to replace existing ones not only in quantity but also in overall price. Titles not carried on GALILEO will be given highest priority for the print collection, with an emphasis on consumer-oriented titles.

Print and Electronic Reference

Houston Public Library has no usage statistics for print reference sources, but the reference transactions at the Central library have decreased over the last 10 years and remained constant at branches. (See Chart 2.)

The numbers suggest a decentralization of HPL reference services not only to branches that offer more resources with online collections, but also to self-service home and office computers. This, along with the eyewitness accounts of HPL reference librarians, has made print reference sources another major target for savings. As with periodicals, the process occurred very quickly in branches. As free and fee information from the Internet became available, librarians were given permission to drop indexes and expensive reference sets that were no longer used. Central departments were encouraged to drop duplicate reference sets in preparation for the transition to a single reference point in the renovated Central Library. Standing order reference titles dropped at Central and branches in 2000 amounted to $65,000. Another $30,000 was dropped two years later.

More recently, as databases that have print equivalents are added to the library's collection, all print copies at branches and all but one at Central are dropped as a matter of course. In the current economic climate, sources cannot exist in both print and online formats. Purchasing an online product requires finding a product of equal value to drop from the existing print or online collection. For example, HPL dropped all but one of its print subscriptions to the *Statesman's Yearbook* and added its excellent online equivalent *SYBWorld*. The library got a manageable quote from Valueline, Inc. for the online version of its popular investment survey, but convincing users and librarians to give up print will be a challenge. *World Book Encyclopedia* may be dropped from the online collection because the library provides access to other online encyclopedias, and the print edition is replaced annually at all of our branches.

Perhaps to the short-term detriment of the online collection, library infrastructure issues have been used as justification for not dropping online products with low use. With retrievals up and budget cuts coming, this practice is no longer justifiable. HPL has begun the process of evaluating databases on a cost per full-text retrieval basis. Databases that do not meet the initial standard of less than $5.00 per full-text retrieval will

CHART 2. Reference Transactions at HPL Since 1991

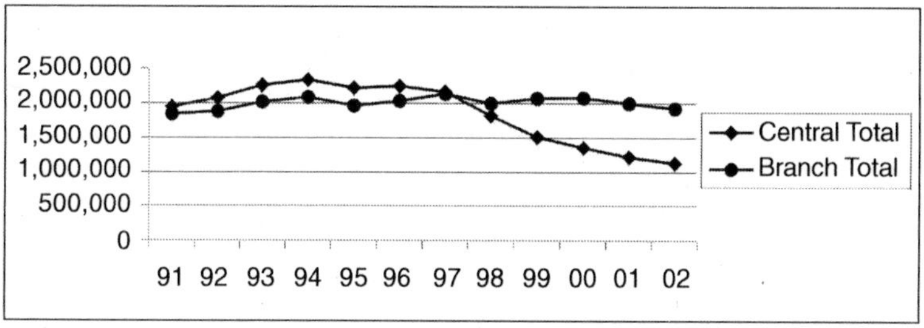

not be retained unless the price can be renegotiated with the vendor. We expect the standard to lower and level off in the next couple of years as our usage returns to normal levels. Furthermore, the holdings of all periodicals databases are being compared for overlapping titles, and databases with the least unique full-text content will be dropped.

Forsyth County Public Library found that staff and patrons clung to the print when online resources were first introduced. To ease the transition, and since funds were available, reference serials continued to be purchased, even if they duplicated online offerings. Over the past few years, staff and patrons have become more comfortable with online, and print duplicates are being dropped because of space and funding. For example, FCPL purchased Gale's *Literature Resource Center* in the fall of 2000. Three Gale reference sets were being purchased in print: *Contemporary Authors*, *Contemporary Authors, New Revision Series*, and *Contemporary Literary Criticism*. With the online edition, it was unnecessary to acquire the print, except that information staff expressed serious fears about losing these familiar print resources. As a compromise, only *Contemporary Literary Criticism* was dropped. However, since the second branch opened at this same time, it was decided that each branch would retain only one of the remaining sets, leaving both sets intact in the system.

Over the next two years, staff became so comfortable with the online product that no one seemed to notice when the two remaining print sets were discontinued in July 2002. This amounted to a savings of $2,200 during FY2003.

Weeding for print and media materials is carried out on a three-year rotation, so that all collections are weeded within a three-year period. Central collection development staff compares statistics for demand

and turnover rate. Report queries are formulated on circulation and last check-out date. Counts of number of items to be withdrawn are compared to the total collection size. The number of check-outs required for removal varies by collection. Withdrawals for low circulation range from 5% to 18% of a total collection.

The biggest change in print weeding since electronic reference was expanded in 2000 is in nonfiction weeding. Even though the size of the adult nonfiction collection outweighed the demand, in-house use was factored in and nonfiction was not weeded heavily. For example, items would have been pulled if there had been no checkouts in two years, and the publication date was more than five years old. Now, nonfiction is weeded if there have been no checkouts in the previous year, assuming the item was added more than 18 months earlier. It has become accepted that Internet products will make up the difference.

Deciding which items to weed is done in two steps. After a list of items to pull is created by Collection Development staff from statistics, the list is sent to the branches for professional Information Librarians to pull the items. They have the right to make a judgment call on the item–keep it or delete it. It has taken a few years to develop a mindset that it is a good idea to let a "shelf-sitter" go. Information staff make notes to Collection Development staff about gaps on the shelves (not enough titles in a subject area), about Dewey ranges that are circulating so poorly that all books are being weeded, and general patron observations. Collection Development staff responds to these notes by tailoring selections and orders accordingly.

However, this is the first year that databases have been evaluated for weeding. Library management hesitated to drop products until a marketing campaign for the remote online collection was in force. Budget cuts necessitated marketing plans to be postponed, and database spending had to be reduced. FCPL is approaching this project using statistics and staff judgment, just as is done for print collection development.

Whereas it has been a fairly simple process to pull circulation statistics for print and media holdings from the online system, it has been a challenge to obtain electronic use statistics. The online system gave statistics only on remote database use, and they have not been consistent enough to be dependable. So, Collection Development staff relied on vendor statistics. Although almost nonexistent at first, they are slowly becoming more reliable and more available. Staff chose number of logons as a comparison point, judging that a logon was most similar to a user check-out. Cost per logon was computed, comparing this with cost per check-out (just under $3.00). Statistics were available only for remote products.

Logons for October through December 2002 are represented in Chart 3. It is rather obvious which product got the highest use.

The statistics provided objective data, but subjective feedback from the staff was important. This was consistent with guidelines for print weeding in which professional staff used judgment in whether to withdraw a book from the shelf, even if usage was low.

In order to keep the budget in balance for fiscal year 2004, it will be necessary to reduce electronic databases by $7,000 (1/7 of the budget). Information staff received usage statistics and was asked to respond to a survey, listed below.

Staff Survey for Electronic Products

- Impressions: What comes to mind when you think of this resource? What do you dislike about it? What do you love about it? What does it do best?
- Ease of Use: How easy is it for staff to use? To explain to patrons? How easy for the patrons who use it most (e.g., students)?
- Frequency of Use: How often do you use this resource? How often do you suggest it to a patron? How often does a patron mention it to you?
- Uniqueness: What other resources have the same information? If this database were not available, what would you use instead?

Central evaluation looked at statistics and at anecdotal information supplied by Information staff. Some interesting patterns developed. Staff responses fell into three general groups:

- "The database has great data, and I use it a lot."
- "The data is good, but I don't use it much."
- "The data is marginal, but I use it often because it's all we've got."

For example, the *American Indians* database from Facts on File had been added in 2001 because of its affordability and information potential to meet the high demand of annual school reports. Print had never seemed adequate–staff regularly indicated that they "needed more Indian books." Electronic usage statistics were low, which was explained by staff comments on the survey. Staff responded that they seldom used this database, even though there was a lot of good information. Reasons

CHART 3. Vendor Logon Statistics

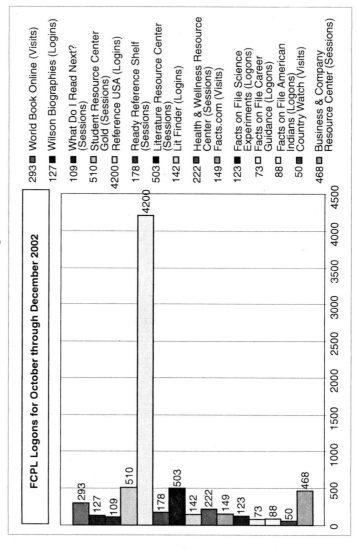

FCPL Logons for October through December 2002

293 ▨ World Book Online (Visits)

127 ■ Wilson Biographies (Logins)

109 ■ What Do I Read Next? (Sessions)

510 ▨ Student Resource Center Gold (Sessions)

4200 □ Reference USA (Logins)

178 ▨ Ready Reference Shelf (Sessions)

503 ■ Literature Resource Center (Sessions)

142 □ Lit Finder (Logins)

222 ▨ Health & Wellness Resource Center (Sessions)

149 ▨ Facts.com (Visits)

123 ■ Facts on File Science Experiments (Logons)

73 □ Facts on File Career Guidance (Logons)

88 □ Facts on File American Indians (Logons)

50 ▨ Country Watch (Visits)

468 ▨ Business & Company Resource Center (Sessions)

given included: the reading level was above students who needed it; adequate information was available in *World Book Online* and general Internet searching; and print was still favored. In requesting this product to be dropped, several staff members asked that more print be purchased. Here was a case where duplication between print and electronic could be avoided by dropping the electronic version.

The final decision was based on both statistical data and staff input. Four databases were dropped, three for low usage and one because of overwhelming staff recommendation, even though usage was moderately high. These cuts reduced expenditures by $11,000, more than necessary to make up the budget shortfall.

Dropping these four databases created funds for new database offerings. The cycle has begun again in analyzing patron needs and available databases. Library management decided to focus on homework support, so a few databases were targeted that would provide help in assignments and could be accessed from home. These are currently under review by library staff and a liaison staff member at the school administration level.

E-Books

For both Houston Public Library and TexShare, e-books have been a part of the collection since the early offerings of netLibrary. Over a two-year period, HPL purchased single copies of 1,861 e-book titles. During the same period, the TexShare collection has grown to 22,839 titles. Among the many reasons e-books have been attractive is that they are one-time purchases. Even when the economy was prosperous, e-books offered the comfort of not having to find the money annually. However, because the service has never taken off in the public's imagination, purchases after the initial one have been made with gift funds designated for the purpose. More bandwidth, more titles, and providing catalog access to e-books have all contributed to increased use of the format at HPL–keeping management optimistic that addressing intellectual property issues and enhancing the users' experience will eventually make e-books a viable format.

Forsyth County Public Library has not purchased e-books. GALILEO offers netLibrary, and FCPL could acquire cataloging for the titles selected through a special state committee. However, there have been no requests for e-book titles and staff reports that patrons do not use netLibrary in the library. In an attempt to promote e-books, the free version of *Riding the Bullet* by Stephen King was downloaded onto one terminal in the library in 2000. Not even one patron requested to access this title.

FUTURE ELECTRONIC COLLECTION MANAGEMENT

Essential in the maintenance of the total collection is the examination of the online database collection annually. Houston Public Library and Forsyth County Public Library both recognize the importance of the following activities for future enhancement of electronic collection management.

1. Improving public use and awareness of electronic selections
2. Collecting better usage statistics and applying them to collection evaluation
3. Seeking funds for new offerings beyond traditional local and state funds

Again, both libraries approach the implementation of these goals based on their unique communities and available resources. System size can be an asset as well as a liability, and HPL and FCPL must use size to their best advantage.

Houston Public Library implemented *HPL powerSEARCH* in July 2002 to make the databases easier to use and thus increase use. In August 1999, a change in the library's remote authentication method gave users the burden of setting up a proxy on their individual browsers. Many schools and business were excluded from HPL services because of their own internal security measures or proxies. The set-up for AOL users was so complicated that many of these users gave up trying to access the resources. Use dropped significantly and remained stagnant. While the statistics were not increasing, increases to the online budget were not justifiable. Furthermore, it was difficult to market a product that was so difficult to use. With the implementation *HPL powerSEARCH*, a remote authentication solution and a multiple database search interface by Webfeat, Inc., full-text retrievals in the first six months were up 65% over the same period of the previous year.

In an effort to improve customer service and online use, HPL hopes to be more proactive in turning resources from print to online in the fast-changing business environment. It's an area where users have begun to make inquiries, and the library should not be far behind demand. The cost of these services requires that several reference librarians evaluate all the products simultaneously and make recommendations for both adds and drops in print or online. A reevaluation of the way business customers use the library will be a necessary part of this process.

In obtaining new funds, HPL would like to lead the way in encouraging the creation or expanded use of local or statewide consortia for buying online material. For instance, three public library systems in the Houston area have separately purchased the same test-taking database. In a consortial environment the database could be purchased for more libraries at a better rate to the individual libraries.

Finally as part of a total collection evaluation, HPL would like to find feasible measurements for comparing the effectiveness of print and online collections. Is comparing cost per full-text retrieval in the online collection to cost per circulation in the circulating print collection statistically or otherwise valid? How do you measure whether an academic or reference title is more cost effective as an e-book or whether purchasing a book in both formats makes sense in some cases?

Forsyth County Public Library recognizes the need to promote the electronic collection. An Information Services staff member who is enrolled in an MLS program conducted a survey of 50 patrons in the fall of 2002 for a class assignment. The survey listed licensed databases and asked patrons to indicate which ones they had used. Averaging the responses, 80% of the patrons had never used the licensed products.

Since funds are not available for advertising and community marketing, library management has decided to focus on marketing the electronic collection to students. Discussion is underway with administrators from the public school system on disseminating information to media specialists and classroom teachers on homework resources available online. Partnering with the school system enabled FCPL to obtain an LSTA literacy grant in 2003 for Spanish print materials. A continued partnership arrangement might provide access to corporate funds for electronic products. Donations of electronic materials would be another integration of formats, since the library also receives print and media donations.

Another option in balancing collection formats as well as the materials budget is to incorporate more free sites into the online catalog. These may replace some print and even some licensed electronic products. GALILEO recently released technical instructions on linking directly to licensed databases rather than users clicking their way through numerous menus and levels. FCPL plans to add these direct links into the catalog.

For example, one of the four databases that will be dropped is a large business resources database. Staff had consistently cited other sources as more useful, especially GALILEO resources. However, logons to the licensed product were fairly high, indicating that patrons were looking for business information. Collection Development staff recognized that patron demand should be addressed in another way. FCPL Collection Development staff decided to pursue adding these direct links into the catalog as a "free" replacement for the licensed business database.

CONCLUSION

Though the current economy makes enhancing online collections difficult, essential online products will continue to appear, and ongoing evaluation of all collections will be vital to a successful library. Houston Public Library and Forsyth County Public Library have only begun what will be a continuous cycle of evaluation of the entire collection. The goal in times of both lean and robust budgets will be making the collection literally earn its place on the shelf or in licensed cyberspace. The addition of cyberspace necessitates that the library re-examine collection practices of the past to see if they are pertinent for meeting users' expectations in today's library. Providing print or online resources because we are familiar with them and not because they are the best available inhibits good service. Likewise, the future may prove that limiting size and age of immediate physical collections with varying methods of online access to archival collections may satisfy more customers at their preferred access points. Finally, using traditional and new methods of measuring both the service value and cost effectiveness of these collections is essential to becoming the most recognized place to access information, read books and have fun learning.

REFERENCES

GALILEO: Georgia's Virtual Library. 2002. Board of Regents of the University System of Georgia. 23 Mar. 2003. <http://galileo.usg.edu/>.

Hoffert, Barbara. "Serving More with Less." *Library Journal*. 15 Feb. 2003: 42-44.

Kovacs, Diane. *Building Electronic Library Collections: The Essential Guide to Selection Criteria and Core Subject Collections*. New York: Neal-Schuman, 2000.

TexShare Library Information: Welcome to TexShare. 2003. Texas State Library and Archives Commission. 25 Mar. 2003. < http://www.texshare.edu/>.

U.S. Census Bureau. United States Department of Commerce. 8 Jan. 2001. <http://www.census.gov/>.

Index

Pages marked with *fig.* indicate figures; those marked with *table* indicate tables; those marked with *chart* indicate charts.

179

BOOK ORDER FORM!

Order a copy of this book with this form or online at:
http://www.haworthpress.com/store/product.asp?sku=5127

Managing Digital Resources in Libraries

_____ in softbound at $19.95 (ISBN: 0-7890-2403-9)
_____ in hardbound at $39.95 (ISBN: 0-7890-2402-0)

COST OF BOOKS _____	❏ **BILL ME LATER:**
	Bill-me option is good on US/Canada/
POSTAGE & HANDLING _____	Mexico orders only; not good to jobbers,
US: $4.00 for first book & $1.50	wholesalers, or subscription agencies.
for each additional book	
Outside US: $5.00 for first book	❏ **Signature** _____
& $2.00 for each additional book.	
	❏ **Payment Enclosed: $** _____
SUBTOTAL _____	❏ **PLEASE CHARGE TO MY CREDIT CARD:**
In Canada: add 7% GST. _____	❏ Visa ❏ MasterCard ❏ AmEx ❏ Discover
STATE TAX _____	❏ Diner's Club ❏ Eurocard ❏ JCB
CA, IL, IN, MN, NJ, NY, OH & SD residents	**Account #** _____
please add appropriate local sales tax.	
FINAL TOTAL _____	**Exp Date** _____
If paying in Canadian funds, convert	
using the current exchange rate,	**Signature** _____
UNESCO coupons welcome.	_(Prices in US dollars and subject to change without notice.)_

PLEASE PRINT ALL INFORMATION OR ATTACH YOUR BUSINESS CARD

Name

Address

City   State/Province   Zip/Postal Code

Country

Tel   Fax

E-Mail

May we use your e-mail address for confirmations and other types of information? ❏Yes ❏No We appreciate receiving your e-mail address. Haworth would like to e-mail special discount offers to you, as a preferred customer. **We will never share, rent, or exchange your e-mail address.** We regard such actions as an invasion of your privacy.

Order From Your **Local Bookstore** or Directly From
The Haworth Press, Inc. 10 Alice Street, Binghamton, New York 13904-1580 • USA
Call Our toll-free number (1-800-429-6784) / Outside US/Canada: (607) 722-5857
Fax: 1-800-895-0582 / Outside US/Canada: (607) 771-0012
E-mail your order to us: orders@haworthpress.com

For orders outside US and Canada, you may wish to order through your local
sales representative, distributor, or bookseller.
For information, see http://haworthpress.com/distributors

(Discounts are available for individual orders in US and Canada only, not booksellers/distributors.)

Please photocopy this form for your personal use.
www.HaworthPress.com   BOF05